Rx FOR HELL

Rx for
Hell

Eileen Stewart

Columbus, Ohio

Rx for Hell
Published by Gatekeeper Press
3971 Hoover Rd. Suite 77
Columbus, OH 43123-2839
www.GatekeeperPress.com

Copyright © 2017 by Eileen Stewart

ISBN: 9781619848542
ISBN: 9781619848306

Printed in the United States of America

DEDICATION

My mother, Audrey, was never allowed to tell her story. No one would listen. As a result of numerous psychotropic drugs coursing through my veins, I walked in her shoes. My arduous journey lasted less than a year; her suffering spanned decades. I take her name in this book so that she may finally have a voice.

CONTENTS

ACKNOWLEDGMENTS

First and foremost, I extend my deepest gratitude to my Aunt Marlyn and Uncle Ross, whose faith in me never wavered. Special thanks to my dear friends Kathy and Arnie Johnson, who gave their unlimited love and support without hesitation, without which I would not have recovered. And to Barb Krauter, Maggie Graham, Angel Zelek, Dani Zimbelman, Diane Rammage, Dell Button, and Robin Kummer, my appreciation for reading countless drafts and providing the encouragement and insight necessary to produce this account.

EILEEN STEWART

INTRODUCTION

Due to the lethal combination of a cruel husband and an astoundingly careless psychiatrist, what started as a commonplace car accident initiated a bizarre chain of events that turned my world upside down. The relentless pain and depression from numerous surgeries, coupled with a host of prescription drugs, spawned a suicide attempt, a felony arrest and potential twenty-year prison sentence, several days in solitary confinement, and almost two weeks in the maximum security wing of a psychiatric hospital.

The miraculous part of this journey was not that He sent angels to walk with me but the very angles He chose. My only comfort during this difficult time was derived from lost souls that never met me and under no obligation or duty, rose above their own desperate situations to help me.

As painful as it was, I relived these events to document my story, in hopes that it will serve others. I can now articulate what it feels like to be held captive by delusions and demons. Perhaps having some insight into another's private hell will prevent loved ones from turning away in frustration. To wage war with an enemy only you can see is difficult enough, but to do it completely and utterly alone – is impossible.

EILEEN STEWART

LIFE WAS GOOD

IT WAS AFTER SIX THIRTY when I walked out of the building which housed TKM Technologies and headed for my truck. My "techie" co-workers and I had all put in the hours. We each had our specialty; I was responsible for software quality, so my job was never done. There was always something more to verify or another issue to identify and diagnose.

I loved my job. As my first start-up; it was the coolest job I had ever had. After eighteen years of software development and test, I had been personally recommended to the budding audio-video conferencing company by one of the founders. I laughed to myself as I remembered how nervous I was for my interview. Among my interviewers were two of the foremost engineer and marketing folks in video conferencing. I didn't remember ever being that rattled for an interview. As soon as I entered the work area, I could sense that these people were more like family. This was far different from working as a consultant for IBM over the last decade.

Since I had no previous experience in that industry, I asked a friend to give me a crash course on video technologies the night before. Despite my nerves, I was able to give them appropriate answers to their questions. I fessed up to my methods and my interviewers were suitably impressed. They said if I could retain the information enough to discuss complex technical issues after one sitting with my friend, then I was the person for the job. After several months in their employ, I was preparing to recruit and build my own team which would hopefully contribute to the company's success.

As I climbed into my big truck, I marveled at how wonderful my life was. I had a new husband, and as far as I was concerned, he was perfect. I met JB when I had to switch flights at the last minute and wound up on his plane headed to Nashville. We sat together and chatted happily. By the end of the flight, we were both convinced that we were soulmates. When I told my father I was getting married, he was understandably upset. We had a short engagement, but as I told my dad, "JB is an engineer and he is Catholic! What more could you want?"

I couldn't remember a time when my father had approved of a man I dated, but he really liked JB. I interpreted this as "it was meant to be." JB lived in Tennessee when we met, but within a few months, he moved to Texas to be with me. We were married a few months later. I had been single for a long time, so I really appreciated how nice it was to have someone to count on, someone to be my partner in life.

Not only did I have a wonderful husband, but I had the ranch I had always dreamt of. I had painstakingly built up the little property into a full-fledged horse training facility. When I bought the property, it was a little house next to a huge mud pit. This was a result of someone's failed attempt to build a pond. Unfortunately, the main design flaw resulted in the bank's inability to contain the water. I used to joke that what I actually purchased was a "mosquito breeding farm." It also included one goat tied to a stake, which they constantly repositioned and resulted in the grass being mowed in circles. The goat was not the only bonus; the property also boasted the inclusion of the all-important chicken, just one.

The ranch no longer remotely resembled the original property. It had taken many years to save up to afford the improvements. But one at a time, each addition was completed. After the stress of all the decisions, and all the money spent, I loved what I created. Now transformed, the place had become part of me. The mud pit was the first thing I fixed, and I needed a bulldozer to come in and level the acre-sized mud hole. Due to the amount of water it held, the contractor I hired actually buried his bulldozer while trying to level it. He had to borrow a larger bulldozer from a friend to pull his free! I smiled every time I pictured it.

Now that same land was a nice green pasture for my horses. I was so proud of my arena with lights, the pristine barn, safe wooden fences, and a wonderful deck that wrapped around the front of the house. It had over an acre of fenced yard for my German Shepherds to play fetch. There was ample pasture for my horses to spend their day contently grazing versus standing in a 10' x 10' stall day after day.

I couldn't wait to go home, slip on my coveralls and head to the barn with my dogs at my side. While performing my chores, I would reflect on the day. My favorite old Quarter Horse, Mister T, was such a good listener. I would lay my head down on his back, my cheek against his ribs, moving with the gentle rise and fall of his rib cage. Communing with Mister T brought me so much peace as I ran my hands over that phenomenal gift God had bestowed upon me. My hands spread over his back warmed by the sun, his fur through my fingers, and the only sound was him graciously chewing his grain.

Mister T's world was so uncomplicated. All he needed was a handful of grain twice a day and a job to do. We would go and work cattle on the weekends; the two of us were a team, doing a sport derived from the Old West. Mister T was the product of generations of careful breeding, and he worked like he knew it. Working cattle made sense to him and he excelled at it.

As partners, the two of us were quite successful in the competitions. There was no day too stressful and no problem so large that a thirty-minute session in the pasture with my little Quarter Horse wouldn't just melt away. No matter what stress I was under, it quickly dissipated when we strode in the arena, taking on the competition. Life was extremely good.

EILEEN STEWART

April 6, 2004
Motor Vehicle Accident

THE SUN HAD STARTED TO slip down in the sky as I pulled out onto the highway to begin my long trek home. Cars, stacked up at every red light, moved at a snail's pace in between. I must admit it was a beautiful drive, even though it did take forever.

As I approached the major traffic light ready to take another highway due north, the light turned yellow. I was second in line and started to slow down to cruise comfortably to a full stop, as did the vehicles in the lane next to me.

Suddenly, out of the corner of my eye, a motorcycle careened ahead and turned into my lane, right in front of my truck. He wound up narrowly avoiding rear-ending the car in front of him that had unexpectedly stopped for the light.

My truck was over 8,000 pounds and I knew if I didn't react immediately and jam hard on the brakes, the rider would be seriously injured. I mashed my brakes with both feet, praying I could stop in time. Before I could let out a breath of relief that I was able to avoid hitting the motorcycle, my vehicle was slammed from behind. My head was thrown sharply forward and then whipped back.

I was dazed for a minute, and then I saw the light turn green. I saw the back of the young man on the motorcycle darting up the on-ramp, his wild hair flying in the wind, oblivious to the accident he had caused.

As he turned left, I reflexively turned my head and watched him disappear. At this moment, a sharp pain ran up the right side of my neck, and I noticed stiffness in my muscles as I carefully swiveled my head from side to side.

"Oh no. Not again!" I mumbled to myself.

I pulled myself together and got out of the truck to exchange insurance information with the driver who hit me. When I got to the back of my truck, I saw the front end of his sedan was crumpled. The young driver was already examining the damage.

"I didn't do anything to your truck!" he said. "I guess I'll just head on."

"Let me get your insurance information," I said automatically as my lawyer dad's training kicked in. "Never leave the scene of an accident without exchanging insurance information," Dad had told me a thousand times.

"Why? Your truck looks all right!" said the cranky driver.

"Yes, but my neck doesn't feel so good. We are going to do this right."

He was right on one thing, though. The back of my truck was fine. Unlike his sedan, whose body acted as a crumple zone to protect the passengers, the truck had a reinforced steel frame with zero crumple zone to minimize the impact of a collision. Great for the utility of the truck when pulling and stopping heavy loads. Dismal for the driver.

Once I was back on the highway, I pressed the button on my steering wheel to dial JB's cell phone.

"Hey, JB? You won't believe what happened on the way home!" I exclaimed into the phone. "This guy on a motorcycle came out from nowhere and I managed not to hit him, but I got rear-ended. I am so glad I was able to stop though; I would have killed the guy. He didn't even have a helmet on!"

JB asked, "Did it do much damage to the truck?

"Not really, but I can already tell my neck is messed up. I don't know what I am going to do about work . . . ."

By the time I pulled into my driveway, my neck was very sore. I staggered through the animal feeding routine, my muscles gradually getting stiffer with every movement. I finally was finished and went into my room to lie down. I alternated hot and cold compresses throughout the evening.

As I walked mechanically to the freezer to get another ice pack, I glanced into the den.

Over the sound of the TV, I said to JB, "I better email my boss and let him know I'll be working from home tomorrow. My neck is really going to be sore!"

Despite my prayers, this was not a minor whiplash which would have been sore for a couple of days and then start to feel better. Three days later I could barely move my neck.

I was sitting in the recliner, doing my best to keep up with email when JB came home from work. I looked up at him when he walked in the door.

"JB, now what am I going to do? My company needs me," I said sadly.

"Oh, come on," he replied. "I am sure the place will be able to go on without you."

EILEEN STEWART

INITIAL TWO SURGERIES

INSTEAD OF DISSIPATING, THE PAIN increased over time. I continued to work from home; I would lie down a few hours and then work a few hours continually until time to go to bed. As expected, the insurance companies ordered their first line of defense, physical therapy. I went to three agonizing sessions a week. When I couldn't tolerate two pounds of weight during traction, it was clear it was time for the next step.

The first test the neurosurgeon ordered was a myelogram to take an x-ray of my spinal cord. They positioned me face down on the table and injected some dye into my spinal canal to better view the nerves and vertebrae in my neck. As painful as it was when they injected the dye, it paled in comparison to the pain I endured when the table rotated until my feet were above my head. I screamed as the dye rushed to the damaged tissue.

The doctor said with alarm, "Hold on, don't turn your head. Hold on!"

I held on with every fiber of my being. I held on so long that when they finally said I could relax; I went into shock. Paramedics came running in with ice packs, trying to bring my heart rate back to normal.

I heard the doctor behind me say, "Yep, I was afraid of that."

I was referred to another neurosurgeon, Dr. Wyatt. He was an older gentleman with closely cut grey hair and deep brown eyes full of compassion. He had a quiet manner and evoked confidence that you as a patient were in good hands. I watched him closely as he scanned the x-ray and reviewed the physical therapy notes.

"I am sorry, but it looks like we are going to have to do surgery," he said somberly. "First, we're going to implant some bone to re-build your neck. We don't want to traumatize you any more than you have been already, so we're going to use a cadaver bone. Then we are going to drill through your skull to attach a metal halo to your temples using four large sturdy bolts. There will be some recovery time at home; you will need to be exceedingly careful moving around until everything heals up."

Dr. Wyatt said I would need help during the day for several weeks. All my family still lived in Maryland where I was born, so I didn't have any family close by. It was another reason that I was so grateful I had found JB. It was so nice not to be alone anymore. Because JB said he couldn't miss work, my father flew down after the surgery to help take care of me. JB's company didn't allow any type of working from home. They didn't even allow flex hours; they actually had to be out of the building at 5:00 p.m.

My dad had visited me numerous times over the years and he enjoyed going to dinner with my friends. My oldest and dearest friends were Kathy and Arnie and Dad enjoyed their company immensely. He was pretty disappointed that I couldn't entertain him this time. Dad looked forward to the evenings when JB was home from work and they would sit out on the deck, chatting amiably while drinking a few cold beers. I would go to bed early in the hopes that the more rest I had, the faster I would heal.

By morning, the sink was full of dishes and it was up to me to pick up after them. I'd look at the pile of dishes in the sink the next morning and think to myself, "Come on, guys. I just had spinal surgery!"

Dad would want to go out in the evening, since I had never mastered cooking. It was something that he never hesitated to remind me of, so it was somewhat of a sore point between us. When JB came home, he would suggest going out for dinner. My dad would light up, and they would both look at me with that same look, the look of dissatisfaction because they knew what my answer would probably be. I simply didn't have the energy needed to get dressed and go out for a meal. The few times I joined them, the increased pain significantly outweighed the enjoyment. It wasn't long before they no longer bothered to invite me. JB would look at my dad and say, "Come on, Pop; I will take you out to dinner tonight." Dad was only too happy to get out of the house.

Dad's visit lasted about a week. He tapped his fingers impatiently on the armrest of the couch as we tolerated yet another repeat on daytime TV.

I said, "Dad, I need to get up and go to the bathroom."

He stood and walked over to the large recliner I was laying on. Suddenly, he pulled the lever to close the recliner. I didn't notice him put his hand on the lever, so I was not prepared for the jerk of the chair when it snapped upright. The recliner threw me forward and I felt a clear snap in my spine.

I said in a whisper, as if speaking might cause more damage, "Oh no."

Dad looked at me and saw my eyes wide with alarm. I didn't move for a few minutes and said nothing. Then, I slowly lifted my hand and cautiously felt my neck.

Dad said hurriedly, "What? What's wrong?"

"I can't move my head, something is stuck. I heard something crack."

"What do you mean you heard something crack? Like what, a bone? Your head is cocked to the left."

Tears ran down my face. "I can't move it at all."

Dad ran into the kitchen to grab the phone. Almost to the kitchen, he said over his shoulder, "Oh my God; I am calling the surgeon right away."

He ran back to me with the phone in his hand. As he reached out to hand it to me, he looked at me with a panicked expression. I hadn't moved a muscle.

I said mindlessly, "His number is written down by the phone."

Dad raced back to the kitchen and I could hear him talking rapidly, his voice filled with alarm.

Dad came back in the room with quick strides. I could see him forcing his body to calm down.

"Dr. Wyatt said that we need to get you to the hospital right away. You are still in a weird position. You really can't move at all?"

I looked up at him with terror in my eyes. I didn't answer. There was no need.

Dad reached out to put his hand around my waist and carefully helped me out of the chair. He continued to try and comfort me.

"Come on, now; let's get you to the car. It is going to be all right."

He slowly guided me to my truck and helped me in.

I'm not sure how great a plan that was, but we had no choice. Dad was unfamiliar with both the roads and my truck, but he was a judge and he knew how to take charge when necessary. He drove as carefully as he could to avoid any bumps or sharp curves. For a man who never stopped talking, it was a very long, silent ride. We were both petrified.

My mind was filled with ominous feelings. What if the bone snapped and had severed part of my spinal cord? What if I was paralyzed in this position?

At the hospital, they lifted me out of the car and into a wheelchair and whisked me to the back to run tests. They brought me back out, and Dad and I waited together for the results. As I was sitting in the wheelchair, I said a prayer that this was not how I would spend the rest of my life. When Dr. Wyatt walked in the room carrying the x-ray films, his distressed expression said it all. This was not good. Not good at all.

"Please tell me you can fix it!" I implored.

Dr. Wyatt looked down at the floor grasping for words.

"Please. Oh, God. Don't tell me I have to have another surgery? The last one was only two weeks ago!" I cried.

Dr. Wyatt reached out and handed me the x-ray exposing the two jagged pieces of the cadaver bone which had snapped. Only half of the bone was in place. The other half had sheared away and was at a forty-five-degree angle jutting into my spinal column. My head was pounding with a migraine. I couldn't move my jaws, and the pain was so severe I wanted to scream. I didn't dare move for fear I would be paralyzed.

I went through yet another surgery and the months of recovery. But, after months of doing everything I was told, the pain was not getting any better and my range of motion was still substantially limited. I went back to Dr. Wyatt's office four months later, convinced the surgery had failed.

Dr. Wyatt's expression conveyed the news before he pronounced his abysmal findings. The second surgery was an utter failure because the new cadaver bone never fused with my natural bone. He sat on the little stool in the examining room, eyes cast down at the floor. He removed his glasses and rubbed his hand down his face. He looked so crestfallen.

I placed my hand on his shoulder and said, "Don't feel bad. I know you did your best."

Dr. Wyatt looked up at me, amazed at the gesture. I didn't blame him; he was an excellent surgeon. I figured he would be hard enough on himself for both of us.

EILEEN STEWART

YET ANOTHER SURGERY

AFTER HEARING THE FUSION HAD failed again, the only solution was yet another surgery. I wanted my life back, and I didn't care what it took. I was in incredible pain. I couldn't ride my beloved horses, and it took everything I had to make it through the work day. I did some research, looking specifically into surgeons who were willing to do what would be considered aggressive surgeries. Surgeons that dealt with complex spinal issues and liberally used hardware to support the remaining bone. I found a surgeon who worked primarily with patients who'd had conservative approaches fail and those who had severe scoliosis.

The new surgeon was quite different from Dr. Wyatt. Dr. Renden was a younger man, energetic and lean with short-cropped red hair. He uttered few words and spoke in fits and starts. After I conveyed the details of the previous two surgeries, he thought for a few minutes while stroking his neatly trimmed beard. Then, he walked quickly over to the lightbox and pointed to the x-ray.

"Since both cadaver bones failed," the new surgeon said, "I recommend we go in and take a piece of bone out of your pelvis. We'll turn you face down on a bed, which supports you on both sides, and it rotates. We'll cut an eight-inch incision and slice away all the layers of muscle on your neck and upper back, which, I have to be honest, will result in significant nerve damage. By harvesting your own bone, we minimize the chance of your body rejecting the graft. The added measure of installing plates and screws to make sure the bone doesn't move and has support while it fuses will provide the greatest chance of success."

"Dr. Renden, I want my life back. I am willing to do whatever it takes," I said with a lot more courage than I felt.

Despite my brave façade, I was extremely nervous about this next surgery. After this, there would be more to follow. Over a three-year period, I would undergo a total of five in-hospital surgeries, nineteen surgical procedures, seventy-four agonizing physical therapy sessions, and one hundred forty-five office visits to a variety of medical providers.

Little did I know, the real nightmare had just begun.

April 13, 2006
First Visit with a Psychiatrist

As a result of the numerous medical procedures and associated pain, I gradually slipped into a deep depression. Two years after my third surgery, my husband and my friend Dee convinced me to go see a psychiatrist. I had made it to forty-three years old, and all of a sudden, I was in need of a therapist—at least my friends and husband thought so.

After several laps around the parking lot, I finally snagged a space barely able to accommodate my truck two buildings down from the doctor's office. I felt a flash of disappointment when I successfully parked the beast, as it robbed me of a perfectly good excuse to skip the appointment. It was an older set of one-story offices, almost like a strip mall. With significant effort, I squeezed my body into the small gap allowed between the other car and my truck to extract myself from my vehicle. Then I walked along the sidewalk until I spotted the suite number above the door.

I took a deep breath and walked cautiously through the door. I had never been to a psychiatrist and had no idea what to expect. Within six feet of the door was the reception desk, with a small waiting room to the left. The room was filled to capacity with adults with wearied expressions and many small children trying unsuccessfully to control their boredom. I immediately counted the adults in an attempt to calculate the approximate time this session was going to take. I had missed so much time from work already with doctor appointments, and this was going to burn up a minimum of two hours.

The receptionist snapped me out of my thoughts by saying, "May I help you?"

After I told her my name, she informed me how expensive this conversation was going to be. I tried not to react when she told me the good doctor charged $360 per hour. Wow! That was like six dollars a minute! While my brain was still processing this exorbitant rate, I robotically took the clipboard and pen and looked for a place to sit down. I considered leaving but then remembered how much Dee raved about Dr. Walden's ability to help her, so I decided to give him a chance.

The furniture was old and well worn, and the scratched corner tables were covered with the requisite pile of outdated magazines chock full of dog-eared pages. There were two small brown leather couches, a dim light on the corner table, and another large arm chair by the receptionist desk. The leather edges of each piece showed cracks from the repeated abuse of people getting on and off and children sliding up and down. I found it odd that the majority of the patients in the waiting area were children.

A man exited the corner office door, said a few words to the receptionist and filled out some paperwork. He called my name and directed me into his office. Finally, I thought. I had waited for almost an hour and a half! Let's hope this guy is worth it.

Dr. Walden was not a tall man, and appeared even shorter with his back curved from age, perhaps a result of spending most of his life huddled over a legal pad taking notes. His clothes were slightly baggy. He wore a pair of heavily creased khakis and a wrinkled button up shirt. He was almost rotund with large jowls, a fleshy face and large smeared glasses. I am not sure what I expected, but my first impression certainly did not give me much confidence.

In his office, there was a loveseat and oversized chair for the patient and an old desk overflowing with papers, files, and numerous thick reference books. Several books were half opened and turned upside down to hold a particular page.

"Hello there," said Dr. Walden. "You are a friend of Dee's. She called me. It was so nice to hear from her. I haven't seen her for a while."

It was clear by the way the doctor brightened that he had a great affection for Dee. The enjoyment in his voice gave the impression that they were more like friends than merely doctor and patient.

"How is she doing?" he asked with a broad smile.

"She is doing well; I see her often."

"So glad to hear it. OK, let me take a look at your paperwork."

I sat there anxiously, until I couldn't stand it anymore.

Somewhat embarrassed, I said, "Well, to be perfectly honest, Dee thinks I am bipolar, but I am certain I am not. My mother did suffer from the disorder most of her life, and my father paid particular attention searching for any possible signs that I inherited her condition. As a matter of fact, he recently confessed that he—since I had made it to forty-three years old without a single incident remotely similar to her behavior—that he was certain I wasn't bipolar. Dad said he was quite relieved by this. I honestly had no idea that he even gave it a thought."

"Did you want to discuss your mother?"

"No, thank you. My mother has nothing to do with the current situation. She has not been part of my life since I was three-years-old. I have just been through a horrific ordeal and I am most assuredly depressed. Dee speaks very highly of you, so I thought perhaps you could help me with the depression. I honestly am fearful of any mood-enhancing type of medications or those which have an effect on the brain. But, I do think that perhaps it is time for an anti-depressant."

"What do you think is the basis that Dee believes that you are suffering from bipolar disorder?"

I thought a moment and said, "Well, I have only known her a short time. Dee doesn't have any experience interacting with me prior to my accident, which was the catalyst for this trying time. I met her when I was brokering the sale of a horse and we became riding buddies. At one point, she mentioned that I reminded her of a family member who suffers with bipolar disorder and is apparently problematic."

"How so?"

I answered reluctantly, "Well, she didn't talk at length about her, but I get the impression that it was something related to her not taking her medication consistently. That is mostly a guess; I really don't know the whole situation. Although I believe Dee means well. However, since she formed an opinion based entirely on this last year, her perception is somewhat skewed."

Dr. Walden seemed to relax slightly and said, "So that is why Dee's conclusion does not concern you?"

"Exactly. My sadness and frustration I attribute solely to numerous surgeries, incessant pain, and the potential loss of my career. On the top of all that is the abrupt end of a lifelong passion. I am sure I have been more emotional in the last couple of years than under normal circumstances."

Dr. Walden went on to ask me diagnostic questions for the next fifteen minutes, after which he concurred with my opinion that I was indeed in the throes of a deep depression. He went on to explain that he was a forensic psychiatrist specializing in children with emotional problems. Many times these children were in the foster care system. Dr. Walden was frequently asked to be an expert witness in child custody cases. I nodded my head as my estimation of him was improving.

Dr. Walden asked, "On your paperwork, it states you need help with depression. Why don't you tell me what is causing you distress?"

I took a deep breath and said, "Two years ago I was involved in a rear-end collision on the way home from work in which I sustained a spinal injury. As a result, I have endured several surgeries, countless physical therapy sessions, and countless doctor appointments. Unfortunately, these have had a significant impact my professional and personal life. It is taking every fiber of my being to hold on to my current job. It is really taking a toll on me."

Dr. Walden looked down at the clipboard.

"You didn't list the medical information on the form."

I carefully stood and reached out with a piece of paper. He took the paper from my hand. It was a spreadsheet listing the date, doctor, and description of each procedure as well as a graphical representation of the timeline. Dr. Walden scanned the document and then raised his head and looked at me with disbelief.

"Wow, I don't think I have ever had a patient summarize procedures like this. It is even color coded by surgeon. Can I have my secretary make a copy of this?"

"Oh, no need; that one is your copy."

Dr. Walden looks at me with a quizzical look.

"It's not that big a deal. I have so many doctors and there have been so many procedures that I find it helpful to just hand them this. It is difficult enough for me to keep it all straight, and I lived it!"

Dr. Walden looked back down and resumed taking the information in.

"At first," I said, "I created the timeline for myself to remember all the medical procedures and dates. Then, I decided why not put it in a form that I would for an executive. I have found that it helps me. It spares me from reliving it all when recounting the surgeries for a new specialist."

Dr. Walden looked up and said sympathetically, "This is an incredible amount of surgery in a very short amount of time."

"Yes, the very reason I organized it on a timeline. The reason the first two surgeries failed was partly due to their proximity. I am pretty sure my body has had enough. The final spinal surgery took the better part of a day. When I finally woke up, there was a nurse sitting in a chair at my bedside reading a book. When I started to move, she grabbed my foot with one hand and put the other one over her heart, saying, 'Thank God, I will go get the doctor!' Then, she ran from the room and out into the hall."

* * *

I started to get more comfortable as we talked, although I found his frequent sporadic breaks to capture notes a little nerve racking. Dr. Walden's expression changed dramatically once he scanned the entire document. When he looked up, his eyes were filled with compassion and he had a new-found respect for what I was going through.

"So," Dr. Walden said, "tell me about your support system. What about family members?"

"Well, actually, I don't have any family close. My company relocated me here over twenty years ago from Maryland, and I never went back. Since I was a little girl, I'd dreamed of being able to afford a horse property, so I could take care of my horses myself. I wanted to live in a house where I could look out the window and catch a glimpse of my horses grazing contently. I could never afford a place like that in Maryland. I do fly up to Maryland as often as I can, at least a couple of times a year. Usually for one of the major holidays, and I try to always be there for my father's birthday in May. There is a large party for him and he wears his kilt every year. It is so cute, with his little knobby knees." I chucked at the mental image.

Dr. Walden mumbled to himself and scribbled quickly in his journal. He then asked, "OK. Tell me about your friends?"

"Well, my career has been forefront in my life since I moved here, and I generally work long hours. Living on a horse property almost guarantees a long commute. The shortest commute I have ever had was about forty minutes each way, but this job is actually over an hour each way."

"Hmm, that is a long day. That doesn't allow much time to socialize. So, I assume that most of your friends started as co-workers."

"Correct. All of my friends that I don't know from the horse competition world, I worked with at some point. The type of work I do has a fairly small base, so these friends come in and out of my life according to the project I am working on.

"I am in a rather technical profession, so co-workers generally are more fun to go to happy hour or parties because we understand each other's work stress and can commiserate. Many times, the happy hours include significant others, but after they have been to one or two gatherings they bail out."

"Really?"

"Yes, I had one spouse tell me he would have more fun if everyone talked in Japanese. Then at least no one would understand the conversation! That is one of the reasons I was so happy with JB. He is an engineer so we can have a reasonable understanding of each other's work."

"Interesting. I guess many gatherings don't include spouses."

"It definitely has caused tension with significant others in previous relationships. But after years of struggling with this, I don't see a way for both parties to be happy. If you don't invite them, it hurts their feelings. However, if they do come to a gathering, then you spend the entire time trying to prevent them from feeling left out."

"So, do some of these co-workers become long-time friends?"

"Yes, even if they are not doing the same project, they can readily understand a particular work issue, or stressful situation. This town is fairly small, so often you wind up working with people you have before. We all kind of circulate. But, work takes so much of my energy that usually my closest friends will be whoever I am working with at the time."

"Any non-work friends?"

I brightened and said, "Well, I have friends through horse competitions. I have competed for many years, up to a national level. But at that level, fellow competitors live all over the country. It doesn't feel that way because you see them almost every weekend at the big shows." I then slumped into the couch. "Well I haven't been able to ride in a long time, so I have completely lost touch with them."

I cleared my throat and blinked several times to prevent the tears. You are not going to cry, I demanded of myself.

Dr. Walden started to ask a question but when he saw me fighting the tears, he stopped. "Well, I am sure that is quite upsetting," he said and then quickly moved on. "Given your current situation, you don't have co-workers or fellow horse competitors for support. You already mentioned Dee; who else is in your support system?"

"JB and I do many things with two other couples. There is Dee and her husband and Laney and Mitch. Laney also rides horses and lives less than a half a mile away."

"Give me some examples of the group activities?"

"Oh, we got together for everything: birthdays, holidays, and many times just because it is Friday. We each take turns hosting; sometimes we would play cards or board games. The most enjoyable parties by far have been the yearly ones, like the Super Bowl. We would have a very large group watching a big screen TV, and the crowd would spill over into other rooms. It would get really festive when there were people rooting for opposite teams!"

"So, the group has common hobbies, and includes the spouses."

I continued. "Yes, Dee and Laney are horse friends. Therefore, we would discuss medical care and training methods, stuff like that. I actually met Laney over ten years ago when she rode by my house with some friends. I was riding in my arena when they went by, so they stopped to ask me if they could work their horses in my arena. I was delighted; it is not much fun to ride all by yourself. We competed in very different disciplines, but still we enjoyed each other's company."

I saw Dr. Walden lift an eyebrow. "Disciplines?"

"OK, there are tons of different equine sports or disciplines. Laney has trained in a sport called dressage since I have known her. That sport is actually part of the Olympics, with the riders on those exquisite Warmbloods wearing the top hats."

"Wow, ten years, that is quite a time commitment. Does Laney do well?"

"Well, she struggles with it. Competition is very hard. People work for many years to excel at a particular discipline. And sometimes, if you change horses, you almost have to start over." I stopped myself and looked at Dr. Walden. "Sorry. When I get talking about horses, it is hard to stop me."

"I would like you to explain; it is the first time that I have seen a light in your eyes. You really love it, don't you?"

"Yes, I do." I dropped my head and cleared my throat.

To prevent me from focusing on whether I would ever compete again, he quickly said, "Please, go on. You were saying that Laney and yourself do different disciplines. So, you don't compete against each other."

"Currently, I compete in a sport called Reining. It has fairly complex maneuvers executed at a high rate of speed. As a matter of fact, I once heard someone refer to it as 'dressage on crack,' which actually isn't that far off!" I said with a wry smile.

"Well do you have much success in competitions?"

"Well, I do pretty well, I guess. I have worked my way up to national level shows in a few of the disciplines. Sorry, that sounds like I am pretty full of myself."

"Don't worry about it. This conversation is definitely lifting your spirits."

Dr. Walden was right; I wasn't slouching anymore. I was on the edge of my seat, head held high.

"What does it take to compete on that level?"

"Well, in my case, I ride Quarter Horse shows. The Quarter Horse Association keeps track of competition results for all year. They have defined a point system dependent upon your standings and the number of competitors in the class. Each sport has a particular amount of points required to compete at the World Championship Show."

"World Champion?"

"Well, that is what they call it. And, technically, people from other countries do compete in certain sports."

"I imagine horses that are successful at that level are very expensive."

"Heavens, yes! The horse breeding industry is in the billions. It is a big deal."

"And you have done this in more than one sport?"

"Well, yes, but I haven't ever won. Honestly, there was really only one sport where I had a decent shot at the title. Long shot aside, it was a great feeling riding into that arena amongst riders of that caliber."

"Thank you for the clarification; consider me edified!" he said with a laugh.

Dr. Walden could now see the lifelong investment, the time and dedication it took to reach my level of competition. I was glad he encouraged me to explain; it made me proud of what I have accomplished. But it also let him know that if the doctors' prognoses were accurate, I would never compete at that level again. Probably never at any level. Now he understood what a devastating loss it would be.

Dr. Walden realized that my mind was going in a similar direction. So, he kept me talking. "I suppose competition at that level is not without its issues. Do people take it very seriously—I mean, personally—if they do not win?"

"Oh, yeah. It can get dicey. Actually, at any level."

Now Dr. Walden seemed genuinely fascinated. "Like what?"

"Well, the best example was back in Maryland when I was on a winning streak. Which actually didn't happen that much," I said with a laugh. "Anyway, I beat one competitor in barrel racing by a fraction of a second three weekends in a row. It was just a local show, but this girl actually snuck out to my rig in the parking lot and unlocked the hitch of my trailer. Fortunately, I was going really slow when it came off, but I was furious!"

"You're kidding?"

"No, I am not. I told you: people put their heart in it. It is not like I haven't lost my share of competitions. Everyone loses at some time or another. It is all part of the game."

"Well, did that incident make you stop competing against her?"

"What? Oh no, if people stopped competing just because they lost or got their feelings hurt, well, there wouldn't be any competitions!"

I continued. "I was astounded that someone would go to such lengths just because I was more successful than she was. Do you know what a terrible accident it would be if my trailer came unhooked and crossed the yellow line? And what a horrific death for a horse!"

"What did you do?" Dr. Walden, realizing we were down a rabbit hole, said, "OK, never mind. Let's get back to your current support system." He looked at his pad. "So, you can probably share war stories with Laney. It sounds like you have been very successful in competition. Is there any rivalry between you and Laney?"

"I only tried her sport a couple of times. But I guess there is a little rivalry, kind of unspoken though."

"Like what?" he said as he lifted his eyebrows.

"Well, a few years ago, Laney invited an Olympian to teach a clinic at her farm. I mean an actual Olympic competitor. Laney was very proud, rightly so. Even though it wasn't my sport, I went over to watch the lessons."

"I really liked the clinician's approach to addressing an issue with a maneuver; she rarely put the horse at fault. Instead, she would give the rider direction and it would all come together."

"Wait—not sure on your point about the horse."

"Oh, sorry. Well, as I said, people really put their heart in it. It is a tremendous amount of work. And hey, we are all human. When suffering a defeat, sometimes it is easier to say my horse has limited ability or that he balked in the show rather than blame yourself. I am certainly guilty of that a few times myself. But you don't learn that way. If you can't take brutal criticism, you will never get far."

Dr. Walden said with interest, "I have never had a patient who competed in equine events as that level. The emotional or psychological facet of winning and losing in that type of event is quite fascinating. Go on. The Olympian, the clinic . . . "

I laughed to myself. I wasn't convinced Dr. Walden was that fascinated, but it was the first time since my spinal injury that I had talked about competition. It was definitely lifting my spirits. I had seriously trained for many years; thus, it was a huge part of my identity. Recounting my accolades made me realize that even if I never competed again, my accomplishments could not be taken away. They were mine, no matter what happened.

Maybe the good doctor was smarter than I initially gave him credit for.

I hesitated a minute to grab the previous thread. "Yes, right. I liked the clinician's style so much I went back to my house to get Mr. T and took a lesson. I am always open to advice from someone of that caliber, different discipline aside. The clinician was well versed in my sport and readily appreciated my gelding's ability. After a long day of lessons, Laney set up some drinks on the deck for a happy hour."

"Well that sounds fine, finding common ground with someone you enjoyed riding with."

"Yes, but it kind of backfired on me. At the happy hour, the people who only rode in the afternoon repeatedly asked me what type of riding I did. They had not seen me before, so they knew it was not dressage. I tried explaining the required maneuvers of reining, but with little success. Finally, someone suggested that I run over to my house and get a video of one of my competitions.

"Fifteen minutes later, I placed the DVD into Laney's machine and stood in the back of the room. The guests huddled around the TV and watched the video. They were really impressed by the sport and difficulty of the maneuvers. However, Laney wasn't very happy."

"Why would that upset Laney?" he asked.

"Well, she had gone to a lot of trouble to put on the clinic and that probably wasn't the way she expected the day to end. After the video, the clinician spent a significant amount of time talking to me. It was clear that hurt Laney's feelings. I guess Laney thought I upstaged her event. I still watch clinics at her house, but my horses stay home."

Dr. Walden wrote some notations in his journal and smiled; he could see how important my horses were to me.

I waited for him to stop writing. "I can only think of one other time I tried dressage. It was at a schooling show or practice show. They held it at the barn where I boarded Mister T while I was out of town competing at the World Show. We scored pretty high. It was really fun."

"Wait. You said you did well in Laney's event, but you were just having fun? Was that what upset her?"

"Oh, I see what you mean. Let me clarify. There is nothing easy about dressage, not at all. But since it was not an event I seriously competed in, I didn't have to worry about my year-end standings. Even one bad performance could potentially prevent you from qualifying for the World Show, or keep you from getting a year-end award. But in that little practice show, there were no expectations and no pressure. I was able to pick the pattern that suited my horse best. I could even have my friend Linda read the pattern to me as I rode. A publication even did an article about it, but just because of the circumstances."

"What do you mean by circumstances?"

"Oh, because I marked so well on a horse that wasn't formally trained for dressage. The publication called me for an interview on my other horse because we made Rookie of the Year in the cow horse association. When they heard that Mister T scored well in dressage, they changed the article. My dad actually had it framed for me for a gift, and it is hanging in the living room."

"Mister T. Isn't that the same one you mentioned before?"

"Yes, he is my favorite. Hands down!"

Dr. Walden wrote some notations in his journal and smiled; he could see how important my horses were to me.

"You said Dee was a horse friend; does she compete in dressage?"

"No, she has no interest in competing. She loves them more like pets. Dee has some gorgeous paint horses she refers to as 'yard art!'"

"OK, so tell me about the non-horse activities."

"Oh, right. JB and I were invited to Laney and Mitch's private wedding in the Bahamas. It was a small wedding party, so we were touched to be invited. I almost didn't go; both of my jaws were still dislocated."

"Oh, my goodness. That had to be miserable. Did you consider not going?"

"Yes, but JB was so excited to go. He had forged a strong friendship with Mitch. And it was Laney getting married, so I had to go."

I waited for him to stop writing. "Laney got pregnant not long after the wedding and Dee threw her a nice baby shower. Actually, it was at the baby shower where Dee told me about you.

Dee was very insistent it would help me, and JB agreed. I got the impression they'd discussed it before."

"Really?"

"It is just a feeling. When I told JB about it when I got home from the shower, he didn't seem surprised at all. Maybe JB and Dee had discussed it before she talked to me. I don't like that they talked about me behind my back, but I am sure they did it out of concern."

Dr. Walden wrote more notes and asked, "OK, sounds like you have a good support system of friends. How is your marriage?"

I made a furtive look at my watch. This was going to be a fortune! Maybe it was just my subconscious trying to avoid his question.

Dr. Walden said. "I know; this is a lot to cover. But this is the first time I have met you and I need a good foundation to build on. However, it has been over an hour, so let's finish the session. We can begin the next session with discussing your marriage itself."

"Great!" I said, somewhat relieved. I needed to think about that question a bit.

EILEEN STEWART

MAY 2006
DR. WALDEN

TWO WEEKS LATER, I WAS back in the tiny crowded waiting room. Almost an hour and a half passed by, but just when I was about to leave they called my name.

Dr. Walden didn't waste any time. Once I was seated on the corner of the couch he said, "Tell me about your marriage."

I hesitated, not sure where to start. Recognizing my discomfort, Dr. Walden helped me out by asking, "Were things good before the accident?"

I answered with my eyes cast down towards the floor. "I have to admit things seem to have cooled off significantly after the miscarriage."

I swallowed hard and looked at Dr. Walden. He leaned back and gave me time to collect my thoughts.

"This is difficult to talk about. Our baby not only had Down's syndrome but a serious issue with his heart. JB didn't even go with me to the amniocentesis and I had to call him at work to tell him the bad news." A single tear ran down my cheek and I cleared my throat. Finally, I said, "I was hesitant to have children in the first place because I have severe migraines. It took a lot of courage for me to agree to try. But once I was pregnant, I was so elated. I couldn't believe I was going to have a baby. I was going to give JB a son!"

Dr. Walden held his finger up and said quietly, "Sorry to interrupt, but what do you mean he didn't go? You went to the appointment all alone?"

"No, no. A friend of mine went. Thank God. She said I should not go through that alone. She had a daughter and remembered how nerve wracking it was to have the test. She actually picked up things at the appointment I didn't see. She could see the expression of the doctor change to alarm when examining the baby's heart. It was evident to her my baby had serious issues. So, when I called her crying to tell her, she wasn't at all surprised."

"So, did JB come right home?"

"Yes, he came right home--and, we sat on the couch crying, absolutely stunned." I cleared my throat again and said, "We were both destroyed; we went from extreme joy at having a son, to devastated. At around five months, I started to feel bad and had a high fever. We went to a clinic, and I had to go through the still birth. My family doctor said it was actually the safest thing for me, and I should still be able to have children. Afterwards I decided that I couldn't go through anything like that again, so I started to talk to JB about adoption. I told him there were so many children already out there who needed homes and a family. We had plenty to offer a child. JB wanted no part of it, and it created a distance between us. Now that I think about it, JB seemed to resent me for losing our son, like I was somehow to blame. I suppose people grieve in different ways."

"So, you never saw a counselor to work through the loss of your baby?"

"No, we both went back to work and tried to move forward. I guess there was a void between us after that. For me to get in an accident and have two years of medical tests, therapy, and five surgeries certainly didn't help our situation. Now, there is an even greater distance between us."

"Surely he doesn't blame you for the accident?"

"I don't think so. Although he is a bit resentful over my job. Mainly about the amount of time and energy I expend."

"How so?"

"Well, not only do I work a long day but I have an off-shore team that I am coordinating, so I have to check email up until I go to bed and as soon as I wake up. In addition, my commute is a minimum of an hour and fifteen minutes each way."

"That sounds exhausting even if you didn't have so many medical issues."

"Not only is it zapping all my energy, but I don't see JB hardly at all during the week."

"What type of hours does JB work?"

"Actually, he is off at five p.m.; I mean exactly. The employees don't have access to the building off hours; they must be out by five. That is probably why it seems so strange to him that I can go in the office on a weekend or stay as late as I need. And, his commute is under fifteen minutes. Boy would I like that!"

"It is readily apparent that you are extremely intelligent and have done well in your career. I am sure you are not that easy to keep up with."

"Honestly, right now I can't even keep up with myself. The pain is wearing me down to a nub. I do what I can at work, lie down, and log in again, lay down, and by the end of the day I am exhausted and in excruciating pain." In a stronger voice, I said, "I can't let this company down, I was so honored they selected me—*Me*—to help build their company. It is absolutely the coolest opportunity I have ever been given. I can't let them down."

"There is only so much you can do."

I heard my phone beep signaling a calendar reminder. I looked at Dr. Walden and said, "I am sorry, but I have to go. I have a conference call I need to join. Thank you, Doctor. You are a good listener."

I got up and walked towards the door.

"Wait; I want you to take each of these once a day. They may help reduce your stress."

Then he tore off two pages from his prescription pad and handed them to me.

I looked down at the prescriptions and asked, "What are they? I have never heard of these."

And so it went, visit after visit and script after script.

AUGUST 10, 2006
DR. WALDEN

TWO MONTHS LATER, I HEADED into the now-familiar office and found my favorite spot. As I walked in, I thought about all the tears I had shed in this office. Dr. Walden followed me with his eyes as I carefully sat down.

After I was settled, I said "I am trying so hard, but I am having an even harder time trying to keep up. On a good note, I finally have a comprehensive explanation on why my neck injury was so severe despite the minimal damage to my truck."

Dr. Walden raised his head from his notes and said, "Oh really? Why?"

"I have already told you how accomplished some of the technical contributors are at my company. I was talking to one of them the other day and he mentioned how it made sense that I was not nearly as safe in my big truck as I would have been in a car."

Dr. Walden looked at me with interest.

"Yes, apparently he did a consultant engagement with NASA and was one of the engineers tasked with minimizing damage to the space station when it docked. He said he was always amazed at how a minimal buffer zone on the bottom of the space vehicle would protect it substantially from damage when it landed. He actually worked through the (v-u)/t, the law of motion, equations of both a vehicle with a significant crumple zone and one without. The former showed the impact curve elongated and the latter was a sharp spike." Seeing Dr. Walden's look of incredulity, I said. "No, really. We actually did the math; his entire whiteboard was filled with equations when he finished."

"Oh, I believe you, but what is the explanation . . . in layman's terms?"

"In essence, the crumple zone on a vehicle is made out of material that allows it to bend or collapse into itself upon impact, enabling the car to absorb some of the impact. Without a crumple zone, the full force of the impact is distributed almost entirely onto the driver. The crumple zone actually increases the time it takes for the vehicle to come to a complete stop, which softens the impact on the driver. My truck is designed to retain its integrity both pulling very heavy loads and stopping those loads. If a normal car hits me directly in the back, given my truck's height, the point of impact is actually the frame itself and the full force of the impact is absorbed by me."

Dr. Walden looked at me with sympathy. He asked, "Well, I know why your work day is so difficult, but how about things at home?"

"Well, JB is still a little annoyed at how much I am working. He definitely thinks I am working too hard."

"Well, jobs can change. Does JB like Austin? He moved here from another state to be with you, correct?"

"Yes, he moved here from Nashville, Tennessee."

"Does he like it here?"

"Well, I think he likes Austin for the most part. As I said in the last session, he has become very good friends with Laney's husband, Mitch. Both Laney and I are very happy about it. Mitch didn't have any friends either. Now, when Laney and I switch the conversation to horse or technical stuff, they have their own conversation."

"Oh, I didn't know you work with her also. I thought you just had horses in common."

"Actually, Laney doesn't work with me. She works at IBM. However, we do similar type of work and can discuss work strategies. That is why we became such good friends."

"It is good. JB now has a friend he can do things with while you and Laney are riding. Does JB like his job?"

"I think JB is pretty disappointed in it. He continually talks about his old job in Tennessee, and I can tell that he looks back on it fondly. Particularly, when he tells stories involving his previous boss; he really liked him. By the way he describes it he must have had a prominent role. It may have not been his position, but it was clear he felt valued. All he does is complain about his current job. I keep telling him to find a job he loves; my salary can carry us if needed. I guess it isn't that bad, or at least bad enough for him to go to the trouble of changing jobs."

"You just mentioned your salary could carry both of you. I assume you make more money than him. Does that bother him?"

"We discussed it before we were married. My type of work simply pays more than his does. JB said he would have to be an idiot to be upset that I made too much money."

"So, you think he is OK with it?"

"No, not really. It is not just the salary; I have an exciting job and work with some extremely successful people. The founders of the company sold their last one for over forty million!"

"Wow, that would be intimidating. Do you ever work with them directly?"

"Sure, I was only employee number thirteen!" I said with great pride. "All the people there aren't rich—but the sound and video engineers are the best in their field."

Dr. Walden nodded his head and wrote a few notes.

Dr. Walden said, "So, I guess JB is quite proud of you, being selected to be part of building something so exciting."

"Well, yeah, I guess. I kind of play it down though. Particularly knowing how disappointed he is currently with his own career now."

"Do you think JB is aware you do that?"

"Yes, probably so. Maybe I should try a little harder," I said almost to myself.

"JB makes a reasonable salary though, right?"

"He makes the same amount he made in Tennessee, but he says Austin is too expensive. He continually talks about how cheap a house would be in Tennessee. So, he views it as if he took a cut in pay"

"So, back to the difference in salary. Do you think it is causing some of the tension in the marriage?"

"Yes, but we discussed it before he moved here, because I have run into that problem before. JB was moving into my house, socializing with my friends and my horse world, and I was afraid he would get lost. I actually offered to sell my ranch so we could buy a place together. That way he wouldn't feel like he was living in his wife's house."

Dr. Walden stops writing notes on the pad and stated, "Wow. That would be a pretty big sacrifice. You said it has taken you years to convert it into a horse training facility."

"Yes, I thought so."

I bet he would take me up on it now, I thought.

"Does JB even like the ranch life?"

"Honestly, no. He often mentions how much easier it would be to maintain a little house with a postage stamp yard. He has made it crystal clear he believes the ranch is too much work. I have to admit he is right. You are tied to a place like that. You can't just pick up and go anytime you want."

"Does that bother you also?"

"Yes, but being able to take care of my horses myself outweighs that inconvenience."

"Horses seem to be a very important part of your life. Does JB like them?"

"Not really. JB had almost no experience with them, so he's somewhat afraid of them. He was astonished to find out how much money they cost. He totally freaked when he realized how much money I spent on trainers and entry fees."

I put my face in my hands trying to stop the tears.

I said in a thick voice, "I guess he doesn't have to worry about that anymore."

NOVEMBER 9, 2006
DR. WALDEN

THREE MONTHS LATER, I WALKED into the office and sat on the little couch, expelling a long breath. I had come straight from work and my neck was on fire. I rubbed my neck and moved my shoulders as I waited for him to start.

Dr. Walden said with compassion, "You look like you are in even more pain than usual."

"I am. I know I am supposed to be resting but it is difficult. My company is counting on me, but I am in such pain I can hardly concentrate."

Dr. Walden picked up a letter from his desk. "Your oral surgeon sent over a note he provided you. Dr. Bower is very concerned about your jaws. The amount of pain and stress you are under is absolutely inhibiting your healing."

"I know. I read it."

"Did you? The part about if you don't rest and keep the stress to a minimum, and I quote: 'you will never recover the use of your jaws,' end quote. I didn't realize that your jaws were so fragile. Why did it take multiple procedures to correct the joints?"

I looked at the floor as my eyes filled up with tears. I waited until the tears stopped and explained.

"I guess I didn't tell you the whole story. My jaws were dislocated for several months before the reconstructive surgeries."

"What? Why?"

"The insurance company wanted full joint replacements which would have left me with severe scarring across both sides of my face. They would not approve the one provider who was able to remedy the damage arthroscopically. So, it was almost eight months before the initial surgery to reconstruct both sockets."

"Good grief! You mean when you went eight months with both jaws dislocated while you battled with the insurance company?"

"Yes, I didn't know they were dislocated right away. The pain in my neck and my migraines were so severe I didn't even realize it."

"I know you never told me that! How did you find out?"

"I went to the dentist and couldn't open my mouth to even allow a small woman's fingers in to clean my teeth. So, he ordered an MRI. When he called me back into his office, he told me both of my mandibular joints were completely dislocated. Both of my jaws were literally hanging on by a thread. They were held in place by what was left of the ligament which supports the socket. The stress and swelling on these joints just below my temples is triggering the migraines and amplifying their intensity. It took several months to convince the insurance company to pay for the surgery, so the ligaments were down to shreds by the time they did the procedure. That is why it took two full reconstructions and several office procedures to remedy the damage."

"Oh my God. I can't even fathom the amount of pain you were in."

"I think my co-worker summed it up best. When I returned to work after hearing the MRI results, he couldn't believe it. My normal working day was usually ten hours or more at that time. My co-worker just looked at me and said, 'You are made of steel! I had a shoulder dislocated once and cried like a little girl until they put it back!'" Remembering this, I attempted a smile, but could not manage it.

Dr. Walden continued. "You can't keep this up. If the job goes, maybe it is what has to happen for you to heal properly. You have literally made a superhuman effort to hold on to your career. But, other things are more important. Did you give this letter to your employer?"

"I will tomorrow."

I let out a heavy sigh.

Dr. Walden said, "I don't think you realize how much you are asking of yourself."

"Of course not. I don't dare think about it."

My feeble attempt at levity had fallen flat. I finally relented and let myself break down and cry. Dr. Walden reached on his desk for a new box of tissues.

EILEEN STEWART

WARNING SIGNS

I SAT IN THE PARKING LOT for twenty minutes until I could collect myself. Then, I put my truck in gear and drove back to work. Day after day of constant pain had taken its toll. I was losing my resolve. The job I once loved so much now only represented continuing severe pain and feelings of eminent failure. I put down the heavy backpack with my laptops and headed towards my co-worker's office. Once there, I sat down and let out a long sigh.

Maggie and I had become good friends. She had a sharp wit and did her best to make me laugh as much as possible. She looked up and followed me with her dark brown eyes. She brushed the dark bangs from her face as she appraised my mood. In a compassionate voice she asked, "How are things at home? You never mention it anymore."

"Well, I hardly see JB anymore. It seems like as soon as I pull in the driveway, he is getting ready to go to bed."

Maggie thought for a few minutes and asked, "What do you mean bed? I thought you usually got home between seven and eight."

"Well, yes, he goes to bed within thirty minutes"

"JB is too young to go to bed so early. I mean, it is not like he gets up at three a.m. What does he say when you come in to go to bed?"

"Well, actually, he started sleeping in the spare room."

"When did this start?"

"It has been several weeks. JB says he doesn't want to roll over and hurt me."

I looked at the floor realizing even I didn't believe that was the reason. Maggie looked at me with skepticism.

"Do you think he is up to something?"

"Like what?" I asked. "I guess it is strange he goes to bed as soon as I get home and gets up real early and is gone when I get up."

"I would agree. I think you should pay more attention. It doesn't sound right to me."

As I pulled into the driveway that night, I glanced at my clock on the dash. It was eight o'clock. The office light was on, but by the time I opened and closed the front gate, the office was dark. I walked into the front of the house near the office where there was no sign of any activity. The computer monitor was shut off and all was quiet. I walked through the house from the kitchen to the den on the opposite side of the house. JB was lying on the sofa with a throw over him as if he had drifted off watching TV. Soon, he rubbed his eyes and announced that he was going to bed.

Oh no, I thought. It is much worse than I thought. It is only 8:45 and he is heading to the spare bedroom.

Was it possible I hadn't paid attention on purpose? I couldn't take any more stress. Christmas was only two weeks away; perhaps the holiday would help to bring us together. We were planning to go to Maryland to see my family. We would be able to spend some time together and we wouldn't have work to worry about.

But any peace the upcoming holiday provided was dashed when my phone rang just a few days later. It was December 12th, a date I will never forget. When I answered the phone, I recognized the Chief Technology Officer's voice. My heart sank as he delivered the very words I had been dreading.

"We are really sorry. You have done a great job. But we are too small a company to accommodate the leave any longer."

I dropped the receiver as the tears rolled down my face. I was devastated. My career was the only thing I had left. I no longer was able to enjoy riding my horses to reduce my stress. Even worse, I would probably never get to ride them again. That thought alone was enough to shake me to my core. I was pretty certain my marriage was on life support and now the job that meant so much to me was gone.

NOT THE CHRISTMAS I'D IMAGINED

I WAS SO HAPPY TO GO home for Christmas. I felt so alone and overwhelmed, certainly my family would lend me comfort. JB was supposed to join me, but at the last minute, he said he had to go see his elderly mother in New York. Well, maybe this would give us some space and seeing his nieces may uplift his spirits. Things had gotten pretty tense. I was sure he wouldn't send me alone unless his mother really needed him. I hoped she was going to be OK.

JB even surprised me with a new audio book. I had become very fond of audio books. They allowed me to rest or endure the migraine and at least have some entertainment. What a blessing! JB said he had selected it especially for the trip. It was the new Grisham novel, *The King of Torts*.

The plane finally landed and I headed down the familiar hallway to baggage claim. I spotted Dad and Bonnie by the luggage carousel. I couldn't put my finger on it, but there was something odd in their expressions. Perhaps, it was the shock of my poor condition. As soon as I hugged my dad, he exclaimed, "Oh, my God, you are as skinny as a rail!"

I realized how long it had been since they had seen me. I probably looked like a different person. My pale, gaunt face, the dark circles under my eyes, and my formerly skin-tight jeans hanging loosely on my hips.

"I told you I have had to be on a liquid diet with all the jaw surgery. And, with migraine after migraine, sometimes I can't keep food down at all."

I looked around to see if there was a place I could buy a bottle of water. I noticed my stepmother was studying me very carefully.

My father had been single for thirty years and then, unexpectedly, he got married. My brother and I were so happy he was not alone anymore, particularly at his age. Bonnie was a retired nurse, which gave us great peace of mind that he would be properly taken care of in his senior years. She was small in stature, just an inch or two taller than me, with a very strong will. My father was no pushover, so it was good she could hold her ground.

"What's wrong? What are you looking for?" Bonnie asked sharply.

"Well, I am taking a lot of medicine and it makes me thirsty. Besides, I have strict orders to not let myself get into too much pain or stress. My jaws were reconstructed twice and the surgeon says I need to relax. Any stress or pain would cause me to bear down on them, which will hinder the healing process. The surgeon said if I don't keep pressure off of my TMJ joints I will actually not recover the use of my jaws."

Bonnie said incredulously, "Oh, that is ridiculous. I never heard of such a thing. Your jaws will heal fine."

I looked at her trying to read her expression. I said with exaggerated patience, "No, it is not ridiculous. The surgeon who performed the reconstructions even went as far as writing a letter to my employer saying it was imperative that I avoid any stress at all. He purported that controlling the pain was key to keep the muscles around the joints from going into spasms. I have been on a liquid diet for almost two years and endured two very painful surgeries to correct the damage. I am going to do what he says to the letter so they can heal."

Bonnie looked at my hand and said, "Open it; I want to see what pills you are taking."

Somewhat confused at her combative tone, I obeyed and opened my hand.

"You have more than three different pills in your hand. Tell me what exactly are you taking?"

Once again thrown by her agitation, I calmly said, "Well, the two white pills are for pain and muscle spasm, which I have been on since the first of the five surgeries. The orange one is new; it is Xanax. I am supposed to take it if I feel my jaw muscles start to spasm. It is supposed to relax me."

"And you are going to take all of them at once?"

"What is going on?" I asked with some annoyance. "I just clearly stated that! I am taking them exactly as prescribed. I have a journal, and I write down the time and the medicine every time I take it. I have so many doctors and so many different medicines that I want to be sure and take them exactly as I should. Sheesh, I guess I should have brought you a copy of the letter!"

We heard a noise and saw the bag carousel had started.

"Well," said Bonnie, pointing to the top of the conveyor, "there are bags coming out. You should wait and make sure you get your bag. You can always take them when you get home."

Without looking at her, I said, "No, I am doing exactly what the doctors said. It will be almost two hours before we get home. It has been five hours since my last dose; I am supposed to take them every four hours. I have to get better; I need to try to get my job back."

I continued to look for a machine with drinks or a water fountain. I walked away partially to attempt to take my medication and partially to get away from the inquisition. My neck was on fire and now my jaws were in spasm, sending pain straight to my temples. I looked back over my shoulder to see Bonnie leaning over and whispering something to my dad. They both nodded, and I could see his harsh look of disapproval.

I took my pills and brought the water bottle back with me. I stood with Bonnie and my dad, watching the bags circle in front of us.

Dad said, "JB said you work too many hours anyway. You need a new job, one where you can spend time with your husband."

I stopped watching the carousel and turned to my father.

"Where did that come from?" I asked. "When did you talk to JB?"

Dad looked at Bonnie and said, "Never mind; here comes your bag."

Something was very wrong, but I had no idea why I was met with such disdain. I was counting on a relaxed holiday to help my jaws heal. On the ride home from the airport, the tension in the air was palpable. It started the minute they saw my frail stature. I knew they would be alarmed at how skinny I was. But instead of them having sympathy for how much I had endured, it was as if they blamed me for something. But, what?

I hadn't talked to them much over the last few months—maybe they were mad about it. But somehow, they seemed to be up to date on everything. Maybe things would be better after a good night's sleep, when I wasn't in so much pain. Maybe I was being too sensitive.

Instead, things progressively got worse. Every time I reached for my purse, my stepmother materialized. I would turn around and there she was.

"What do you need from your purse?" Bonnie asked. "What are you doing now?"

"Bonnie, we have been through this. It is time to take my medicine."

"You just took some pills a couple of hours ago. I watched you!"

"Yes, I did. But they were different than this one. Bonnie, I have shown you my journal where I log every pill I take to ensure I am taking it as prescribed. I have shown you the prescriptions. I don't know what else to tell you."

Each time I saw the disapproving look, I assumed since she had spent most of her life as a nurse that she was just making sure

I didn't get hooked on the narcotics. I was sure she had witnessed many people who were given prescribed medicine and wound up addicted. So, I did everything possible to alleviate any doubt.

I decided to become proactive and let her know every time I took any medicine. That way, she would know that I was not trying to do anything underhanded. I would show her each pill I took and had her watch me write it down. I had a journal filled with page after page of entries. Each line had the date, time, medication, and the dosage. My attempt at full disclosure was to no avail. If anything, it had the opposite effect. She became more and more aggressive. I had no idea what to do.

I was filling my glass of water at the sink. Bonnie was right in front of me. Somewhat startled by her stance, I immediately backed away from her. Having no idea what she was going to do, I turned and walked towards my purse.

"Bonnie, I have explained this over and over. I have those medications for the pain; I write it down every time I take one. I have emptied my purse and shown you every prescription. I showed you my journal where I track every pill I take! What on earth do you want from me?"

Nothing I said mattered. What was going on?

"Stop it, Bonnie!" I said as she reached out for my purse. "For God's sake, I'm not supposed to get stressed. Stop. You are not taking my medications. I need them to heal!"

My dad, hearing the altercation, jumped up from his recliner and strode towards me. I grabbed my purse and held it protectively behind my back, using my other hand to shield my face. Dad was getting closer, his fists clenched and his face red with anger.

"Get her purse," Bonnie yelled. "Take those damn pills away from her! She should have been off the pain medication months ago. JB told us repeatedly she wasn't really in pain. I believe him. She is a useless addict. She is killing herself!"

My father and I locked eyes. I turned quickly and ran into the living room. They both kept coming after me. Now I was cornered and I didn't know what to do. Bonnie had my father all riled up and he had been drinking since early afternoon. I clutched my purse as if it was my lifeline—because it was. I had been through eighteen months of surgeries and procedures and I believed every word the surgeon said. I would not recover use of my jaw if I did not do exactly what he said.

My father continued advancing towards me. Oh my God, I worried. Is he going to hit me?

It was not something he would normally do, but he was so angry. I had never seen him like this. No matter how minute the chance, I couldn't imagine the damage to my jaw sockets if he hit me.

"You give me those pills now!" Dad demanded.

I held my hands close to my face in an effort to protect my jaws. He had to see the fear in my eyes; why wasn't he backing off? He was just a few inches in front of me.

What was wrong with everyone? Why were they acting this way?

"Mac," Bonnie ordered, "listen to me. You get them away from her this instant! I will not have a junkie in my house!"

Dad reached for the strap of my purse, his face was beet red. This wasn't good for either of us.

I had to snap him out of it. I felt like I was fighting for my life.

"If you hit me, old man," I threatened, summoning up all the courage I could, "I'm going to hit you ten times as hard!"

At that, Bonnie shoved her arm in between us.

With her finger in my face, Bonnie screamed, "That's it! You get out of my house!"

When I saw that Bonnie's movement had distracted my dad, I fled for the door. Bonnie slammed it behind me and I heard the slide of the deadbolt.

AUNT MARLYN

ALONE, OUTSIDE IN THE DARK, I sat on the frozen ground, hugged my knees and cried. *What had just happened?*

I sat there and recounted the events. I was stunned; nothing made sense.

I looked back at the bright red door and the green wreath with Christmas candles and holiday lights which just a few hours ago were so inviting. Yet now, I was sitting on the ice-covered grass, out in the middle of nowhere. Bonnie was a nurse; if she really thought I was an addict, shouldn't she have tried to help me?

A few minutes passed. I sat there shivering, wiping the tears away before they could freeze on my face. Then, the door opened and Bonnie tossed my luggage on the front porch.

"I am in the middle of nowhere; at least take me to a rental car place."

She said nothing and slammed the door. I grabbed my phone from my purse and started dialing.

I was at least an hour from anyone I knew. Then I remembered Bonnie's sister. Thank goodness she lived less than five miles away in the same rural area. I had seen Evie many times over the last thirteen years while my father was married to Bonnie. I always enjoyed my time with her; she had a razor-sharp wit, steel grey hair, and enormous blue eyes. She was feisty and full of life. I was elated when I saw her teal green Buick pull in the driveway. I grabbed my bags and ran to her car.

I didn't know what to say. I was so embarrassed. I kept quiet during the fifteen-minute drive to her home. Evie was very kind and, once we arrived, showed me where I would be sleeping.

I had a fitful night with very little sleep. The next morning, I asked Evie if she would take me to the rental car place. We drove there in silence. After forty minutes, we pulled in to the parking lot. I hugged her tightly and stepped out of the car. She reluctantly drove off.

After I had secured the rental car, I called the only two of my family members who were still willing to speak to me: Aunt Marlyn and Uncle Ross. Aunt Marlyn was my father's only sibling. I had grown up close to her, and although she never tried to assume the role of my mother, she had always been there to support me. I picked up the phone and dialed her number, suffused with fear that she would turn me away. To my great relief, I heard her gentle voice say, "Just come on over, honey. We'll be here."

Just like that—no accusations, no demand for explanations—just a simple invite. How wonderful!

On the drive to their house, I kept hearing the awful things Bonnie had said. Over and over, I heard Bonnie saying, "She is not in pain; she is just a junkie!" I had never had such an awful fight with my father. A fear started building that maybe they were right.

Oh my God, what if I am a junkie?

They seemed so certain.

I continued to reach for some explanation, some justification for their hostility. It didn't make any sense.

How in the world would Bonnie have any idea what medicine I was taking or how much? I hadn't seen her in almost a year. What was going on? As I thought about the comments, I realized they all were rooted in JB's reports.

How could I refute the unrelenting statements JB had planted in their minds?

Obviously, only JB's claims were to be trusted. I thought back and realized how many sentences from my father or Bonnie had started with either, "Well, JB said . . ." or "No, we asked JB and it was not that way at all."

It made me wonder just how often he had called them.

Why didn't he ever mention these conversations? In my desperation to heal, I had totally withdrawn. I didn't have any energy left to hold an enjoyable discourse. As I thought about it, it had been several months since I had really spoken with the outside world. My entire life was focused on pain and my unending struggle to relieve myself of it. I had stopped trying to converse with people at all. I knew they had to be tired of hearing how terrible my days were. They had to be. I was sick of hearing it myself! Each time I hung up the phone after talking to someone, I would feel drained. So, over time, I had stopped answering the phone or returning messages. As a result, I had utterly and completely depended on JB. He had been my solitary link to the outside world, and for the first time, I realized what a precarious situation I was in.

I arrived at my Aunt Marlyn's house and she met me in the driveway to welcome me. Aunt Marlyn had wavy silver hair curling back from her face with alabaster skin and delicate features. A gentle creature with bright blue eyes and a quick smile, she had a timeless beauty. She gave me a wonderful and warm hug. I braced myself for comments on how skinny I was, but she offered no commentary on my appearance. I stopped just inside the doorway and basked in the warmth of their lovely home. I took a few minutes to enjoy the sight of the beautifully decorated tree, lighted candles in the windows, and joyful Christmas decorations on every surface. Aunt Marlyn gently walked me over to the dinner table covered with appetizing dishes. Almost in a daze, I slowly sat. My mind reeled as I grappled with the events of the last twenty-four hours. I was sure they also had questions, but they kindly allowed me to unwind. We chatted amiably and enjoyed our meal.

Uncle Ross was a very intelligent and knowledgeable man who could converse on a wide range of subjects. He was tall with a sturdy build and wide shoulders. Age had also turned his hair silver and had shaved a few inches off his once six-foot-two frame, but he was still a man who commanded respect and carried himself with pride.

It was so comforting to be in their home, I felt at peace for the first time in a very long time. Merely being around them and their normal activities—fixing dinner, setting the table, watching a movie—was wonderful. They clearly still believed I would find my way back, which meant so much. Their belief in me was what allowed me hold on to that last shred of faith in myself.

We would prepare every meal together and sit at the table and talk. I knew on some level that I wasn't always making sense, but they patiently listened anyway. They didn't yell at me to stop taking my medication, or repeatedly tell me what JB had told them. They would casually watch me when I was taking medication, and while I was putting a notation in my journal. They would trade knowing looks when I wasn't making sense, but they had enough faith in me to realize it was the side effects and interactions of the myriad of drugs coursing through my veins.

DECEMBER 24, 2006

IT WAS CHRISTMAS EVE, AND I couldn't believe it. What a tough year this had been. But I had to look forward, so I decided to go down to Aunt Marlyn and Uncle Ross's basement to use their computer to check my bank accounts. It was becoming clear that my marriage might not survive and I needed to start making Plan B. I sat down to log in to my bank online, but it kept giving me an error for invalid password.

I dialed the phone, assuming it was a software glitch. A polite voice answered, "Bank of America, how can I help you?"

"I can't get into my account. Can you reset my password please?"

I heard typing in the background. "I am sorry. There has been activity on the account. I am not sure you still have rights to deposit or withdraw on the account."

I shook my head. No, this had to be a mistake. After I answered all of their security questions correctly, the bank finally reset my password. I logged in to my account. When the balance summary filled the screen, I froze. I was shocked to see that the $27,000 remaining from my accident settlement was gone. The balance was less than a hundred dollars! I quickly scanned the summary to find the transaction that radically changed the balance. I saw one transaction with a lump sum. I slid my eyes over to identify the account it had been wired to. Oh, my God. It was JB's personal account.

I hurriedly dialed the phone again, and heard a polite voice say, "Bank of America, how can I help you?"

"Yes," I said, forcing my voice to be calm, "someone has taken all the money out of my joint account with my husband and I need to reverse that transaction."

"Yes, ma'am," the voice said. "I see the transfer. It was done online."

"I understand, but I didn't do it." I rubbed my temples, feeling a migraine rapidly approach. "How can I get the money back?"

"Did someone else know the password?"

"Well, um," I stammered, "yes. My husband"

"I am very sorry, but if someone else had the password, there is absolutely nothing you can do."

I was stunned. I just held the phone to my ear and listened to the dial tone.

Slowly, I hung up the phone.

"What do I do now?"

I walked up the steps like I was going to an execution. I reflexively walked into the living room as my aunt and uncle followed me with their eyes. I collapsed on the sofa in tears.

"It's over," I said to no one in particular. I buried my face in my hands, sobbing inconsolably.

Hearing the sobs, Aunt Marlyn came over and sat down beside me on the couch. She had never seen me so utterly defeated. All my resolve had vanished.

"Don't give up, Audrey!" she said as she slowly stroked my hair. "Whatever it is, you can beat this."

"All the money is gone; there is nothing left. I don't have a job; what am I supposed to do? I will lose the ranch."

"That can't be—you don't think—JB?"

I nodded as the tears ran down my face. I said between sobs, "I know he did! It shows the money was transferred from the joint account and transferred all the funds to his personal bank account."

Aunt Marlyn hesitated, started to talk, and stopped herself.

I turned to look at her. "What is it?"

Aunt Marlyn cast her eyes down and said with embarrassment, "I should have told you this earlier, but JB also called us several times. He said you were hooked on drugs. JB said the way to handle you is to just get up and walk out when you were talking, so you wouldn't be the center of attention."

My heart sank. JB had tried to turn them too. "He said what? Is that why you got up from the table yesterday in the middle of my story?"

She looked at me with tears welling up in her eyes. "Yes, I am ashamed to say I did; but then I came back. It seemed so cruel."

I started crying again and sank lower in the couch.

"Can I see those medications?" She saw the fear flash in my eyes. "I just want to know what they are giving you."

I trusted Aunt Marlyn with my life, so I complied. I mechanically walked into my bedroom and grabbed the large plastic travel bag containing all my prescriptions. She followed me in and sat on the bed. I said the name of each one as I put them one by one in her soft warm hand.

"Concerta. Cymbalta. Imitrex. Phenergan. Relpax. Trazadone. Wellbutrin. Abilify. Xanax. Carisoprodol. Lortab."

Aunt Marlyn looked at each label as I handed her the vials. She verified they were prescribed within the last thirty days. I then reached for the journal on the night table and opened it. Her eyes moved back and forth, page after page. Each scribbled line was comprised of the date, time, and the medication with the dosage. She slowly shook her head.

"What?" I asked.

"I can see you are taking them as prescribed," Aunt Marlyn answered. "But my God, that is a tremendous amount of medication! Also, these are from three different doctors. Do they know what the other is prescribing?"

"Yes. One is the spinal surgeon; one is the maxillofacial surgeon and the rest of them are from the psychiatrist who I started seeing in April. The surgeons send their notes to the psychiatrist so that he can ensure taking all of them is OK."

With alarm in her eyes, she said, "Have you been taking *all* these medications since the surgeries?"

"No, the only ones I am familiar with are the Imitrex for migraines and Phenergan for nausea, which I have taken for fifteen years. The Lortab and the Carisoprodol are for the pain and muscle spasm from the jaw and spinal surgeries. So, I have taken them for several years. The rest is all new."

Aunt Marlyn regarded the pile of prescription bottles on the bed. "That means most of them are from the psychiatrist. Do you know what they are all for?"

"No. It seems like Dr. Walden discontinues and adds them every time I see him. Sometimes, I go to the pharmacy and they have stuff that he didn't discuss with me."

Aunt Marlyn's sympathetic expression rapidly changed to concern.

"Aunt Marlyn, do you think I am a junkie?" My eyes filled with tears.

She gently grabbed my hand and patted the bed beside her. "No, Audrey, I don't believe that for a minute."

"Bonnie sure does!"

Aunt Marlyn suddenly realized something. "Wait. I don't really think she does."

"What—what do you mean?"

"Something has been nagging at me and I just realized what it is. Bonnie's reaction doesn't make any sense. It seems to me anyone with an advanced degree in nursing would get someone help immediately if they thought they were an addict. If Bonnie truly believed what she said, shouldn't her reaction have been to take you to a hospital or rehab?"

I slowly nodded my head as I processed her theory.

"Didn't you think that was odd?"

"Well—I guess—everything is so messed up. I guess I don't trust my perception of things anymore."

"This whole situation scares me to death. All this medication could have dire consequences. On top of that, JB has stolen your money and is apparently calling people and telling them awful things about you." Aunt Marlyn grabbed me by the shoulders and looked into my eyes. "Audrey, I need you to fight! I have known you your whole life . . . fight! I have never seen anything stop you. I can't—no, I refuse—to let you quit! Think! Think! The money is gone, but go save your ranch and whatever is left!"

Aunt Marlyn stood and strode over to the phone. She grabbed it and handed it to me. "Call the airlines; tell them you need to get home tonight!"

EILEEN STEWART

January 9, 2007

I SAT IN THE ALL-TOO-FAMILIAR waiting room at my psychiatrist's office. After what seemed an eternity, my name was called. I hurriedly walked through the office door and straight over to the couch. I started talking before I was even seated.

"Doc, you won't believe what type of holiday I had. I mean it was awful! It was—well, you just won't believe—"

"You seem agitated today," Dr. Walden interrupted. "You are talking too fast."

"Well yes—I am incredibly upset."

"Slow down."

"What? OK, fine." I took a couple quick breaths. "You can't believe the horrific Christmas I had." My eyes filled with tears. "My family was acting so strange. They all think I am an addict!"

"OK, take it easy."

"No, please listen to this. I showed my stepmom my journal where I log every pill that I take. I am extremely careful. Every single time I reached for my purse or filled a glass of water, Bonnie was there in a flash, like out of thin air!"

I looked up and took note of his expression. Normally, Dr. Walden had a kind and sympathetic expression, which made him easy to talk to. This time he looked skeptical, almost stern. His entire demeanor was different. Something was off.

"Oh, and not only did I have the worst Christmas of my life, but I was laid off right before I left for Maryland."

"I know. JB told me."

That stopped me cold. "What? When did you talk with him?"

I tried to conceal my annoyance. I was growing very weary of having my feelings and opinions negated by something JB had told them.

"Well, JB was quite concerned. He called when you were in Maryland. He said you were so out of control that your father had to throw you out of the house. He said you were overmedicated, and your pupils were dilated. JB says he is afraid for you."

My annoyance quickly gave way to fear. Now my doctor was taking direction from JB. This was not good, not good at all. I felt the panic welling up inside me.

"Hold on, you are MY doctor. I don't want you talking to JB. During any of the conversations did he mention that he drained the joint bank account over Christmas? I called the bank; they said I have been removed from the joint accounts. Something is going on here."

"Well, your father agrees with JB."

It was abundantly clear that Dr. Walden was not listening to a word I said. I wanted to scream, but I had to get a hold of myself. I hadn't seen Dr. Walden in two months. JB must have been calling him regularly. I suddenly realized that the missing money wasn't my biggest concern. I hadn't broached the subject with JB because I wanted Dr. Walden's opinion on how to approach it. That money was gone. It was my word against JB's and clearly no one believed anything I said. I needed to let that go and focus. I was in serious trouble here. I warned myself to tread very carefully. I took several deep breaths.

"When did you talk to my dad?"

"Well, your father has been talking with JB. They are both very concerned about you. JB says you refused to take the Abilify. He said when you wouldn't take it he resorted to putting them in your protein shakes. Maybe that is the reason for the erratic behavior. He wasn't there to take care of you."

I did my best to quell the anger that was building inside. "Doctor, we discussed this when you first met me. I am not bipolar! I am very depressed; that is all. And, I don't think the Xanax is helping. As a matter of fact, it feels like it might be making me more agitated. Look, let's deal with the pain and depression and then we can examine the bipolar issue."

"Listen to yourself. Do you know how paranoid you sound?"

"Um, well, I am paranoid because my doctor, my husband, and my family are all talking behind my back."

It was readily apparent that nothing I was saying was making a dent. I continued to take deep breaths and forced myself to speak slowly. I needed to get through this session and then figure out how to handle this. But for now, I needed to do whatever was necessary to remain calm.

"JB told me about your mood swings, paranoia and hyper spending even before Maryland. That is why I prescribed the Abilify and he picked it up for you."

"What? You are—you mean you are prescribing medications, without even talking to me? I haven't talked to you since the beginning of November."

The pieces of the puzzle were now coming together. JB was talking to Dr. Walden behind my back and then picking up the new prescriptions without telling me. *JB said I was just forgetful, but it wasn't me!*

"There is no need for alarm."

The hell there isn't!

My safe haven had vanished. It was replaced with a stressful place where I would have to mentally tiptoe instead of receiving consolation. One ill-chosen phrase, said in a particular manner, or some behavior reported to him out of context and Dr. Walden would write even more scripts. *I can't keep track of what I am taking now!*

My mind was clouded with so many thoughts. I had to get a grip. I reached for a Kleenex in an effort to buy myself some time to think. *How many times has JB called him? When did it start?* I tried to think back to determine when Dr. Walden's demeanor changed. He carefully observed my every move, weighed each word.

In a vain attempt to break the tension, I said flippantly, "Doc, the reason I am talking fast is because you are like six dollars a minute – literally!"

But this time Dr. Walden didn't appreciate my humor. On the contrary, he looked annoyed. He must have thought I was not taking this seriously enough. Oh my God, what could be more serious?

I reminded myself to slowly breathe in and out. "Don't worry; it is going to be OK. I do request that you please don't talk to JB anymore. I am happy to come in as often as you want."

This was so disconcerting. Dr. Walden was convinced I was mentally unbalanced and believed he had corroboration from my family. Whether it was a misrepresentation or not, the damage was done. *What a mess!* My mind was racing, but I needed to calm down. I continued to concentrate on breathing slow deep breaths. I warned myself not to show any type of behavior that would have Dr. Walden reaching for his prescription pad.

And then the startling realization hit me. All the powerful medication I was dutifully taking had been prescribed based purely on the words and perceptions of another person. To make it even worse, it came from another person with their own agenda. The massive wall JB had so carefully constructed, block by block, over the last few months was suddenly visible. I could finally see the impenetrable barrier that stood between myself and those that I held dear. But it was too late, the damage was done.

As I drove home from Dr. Walden's office, so many things ran through my head. *How in the world was I supposed to remedy the situation? What do I do now?*

I pulled into the pharmacy to get my normal post-surgical pain medicine. The friendly pharmacist greeted me, but then looked puzzled when my medication was not in the bin. She walked over to the computer and started typing. Her expression changed as she read the notes on the screen.

"I'm sorry, there is a note here stating Dr. Wyatt is refusing any refills. I guess he wants you to go in and see him."

My heart sank. "This can't be happening," I said under my breath as I quickly turned and walked towards the exit.

EILEEN STEWART

JAN 12, 2007
DR. WYATT

I RAISED MYSELF UP ON THE examining table with the little thin piece of white paper crunching under me. I told Dr. Wyatt about how I had such a terrible Christmas. I was extremely depressed. What should have been a comforting time with family had been a nightmare. I also informed him that I had been laid off the job shortly before Christmas. Dr. Wyatt's expression filled with compassion as he watched the tears streaming down my face.

Dr. Wyatt said, "I think you should discuss getting back on the Wellbutrin with Dr. Walden."

"Maybe that is a good idea; actually, I never told him to discontinue it. I will leave a message for him to refill it." I cleared my throat. "Why did you deny the refill for the Lortab?"

Dr. Wyatt looked down at his feet. "Well, JB said you are not actually in any pain. He is concerned you are hooked on the medication."

I tried very hard to conceal the anger building inside. "What?"

Calm down, I warned myself. JB had now convinced him that I was an addict, my own surgeon! Somehow, I had to convince Dr. Wyatt of how badly I needed the medication for pain without sounding like I was just desperate for a fix.

Dr. Wyatt continued, "He said your father and stepmother have the same concern."

My heart sank. If I can't get out of pain, my jaws will not heal. My attempts to prevent the sobs were futile. Dr. Wyatt asked if I wanted a few minutes to collect myself. I shook my head.

After a deep breath, I said with more calm than I felt, "Please, Dr. Wyatt. How does anyone know how much pain I am in but me? You know better than anyone the nerve damage and trauma to my neck. You saw the letter from the surgeon who reconstructed my jaw twice. It clearly stated I needed to take great care to ensure my jaw heals. Dr. Wyatt, I am begging you. If I don't control the pain, it turns into a migraine and then I clench my jaw. Please do not do this to me. And, please stop talking to my husband. JB drained the joint account. He is up to something. I am your patient, not him."

To my great relief, Dr. Wyatt agreed to refill the normal pain medications. As soon as I got back into my car, I called Dr. Walden's office.

When the secretary answered the phone, I asked to speak with Dr. Walden. She said he was not in the office at the time, so I asked if she could put a note in my file that I wanted the antidepressant refilled. She asked me to wait for her to pull the file.

She replied, "I am looking at your file and I am a little confused. It says right here that on the fourteenth of December, your husband called and told Dr. Walden that you asked to discontinue the Wellbutrin."

"I am sorry; that must be a mistake."

"No, the file even has the exact phrase JB used. The actual verbiage JB used was 'Audrey said the Wellbutrin was utterly useless and she wanted it discontinued.'"

I said hastily, "Well, um, JB must have been mistaken. Please, I need the Wellbutrin back."

"OK, let me page him and ask him if I can call it in."

"Please make sure you contact him today. I just saw Dr. Wyatt and he said that he thought it was imperative that I start taking it again."

January 19, 2007
Depression Becomes the Victor

I COULDN'T FIND MY PHONE, SO I grabbed JB's on the way to my truck. JB was at work and wouldn't need it. I texted him that I had his phone so he wouldn't look for it. I needed to go to the feed store to get some shavings for the stalls. When I was finished at the feed store, I climbed back into the truck. I looked down to put the key in the ignition and noticed JB's phone was flashing, indicating there was a voicemail message.

I didn't think much about it until I pulled into the driveway. Then, it occurred to me that JB was aware I had his phone, so he might be trying to reach me. I listened to the message, but it was the voice of a girl that I didn't recognize. I thought that I must have been mistaken, so I played the message again, listening more carefully. I listened in astonishment to the words which will be ingrained in my memory forever. The message was from a girl who flirtatiously said, "Sorry I was so silly and horny the last time we spoke, but you know how I get when I am ovulating."

The girl was giggling as she left the message, so I listened to the message two more times time to verify I heard the correct words. *This can't be for JB, right?* I checked the call log on the phone and my heart skipped a beat. The number matched a call from Birmingham, Alabama, and there were many calls logged in the last few days. The message was indeed for my husband. So, not only had the marriage been waning, he was in the middle of a torrid affair. That was it. We had lost our baby three years ago and now he was trying to get another woman pregnant. *While he's still married to me! Is that why he didn't go to Maryland with me at Christmas? So he could get his mistress pregnant?!*

Something snapped in my head. It was the infamous last straw and my life as I knew it was officially over. I had no job, an emotionally vacant husband, my family no longer wanted anything to do with me, and almost every friend I had had stopped calling months ago. I set the cell phone down, calmly walked into the bathroom and grabbed the bottle of Xanax from the counter.

I opened the vial and saw the little orange pills brimming to the top. I had recently filled it, so there had to be at least one-hundred pills in the container. I set the cap on the counter. I then looked in the mirror and watched as I dumped the entire bottle of pills in my mouth. I just stared at myself in the mirror. Once I swallowed the pills, my facial expression changed from utter sadness to contentment because I knew my suffering was finally going to end. I didn't know what was in store for me next, but it had to be better than the excruciating emotional and physical pain I had been in for so long.

Of course, I still had one problem: I was raised Catholic. So, I went over to the bed and lay down, starting to say Hail Marys in the hopes God might forgive me. I kept saying the prayers until I couldn't remember the words anymore. I heard JB calling for me. He must be home from work; it must be past five . . . . I wondered how much time had passed. I took the pills around three o'clock I thought, as I faded back out of consciousness.

When I didn't answer, JB came back in to the bedroom and tried to wake me. I was almost gone; all that was left were my auditory faculties.

I clearly heard the agitation in JB's voice as he said, "This is just great; now what do I have to deal with? OK, here we go . . . ," he said as he slipped his hands under my shoulders to pick me up.

He immediately realized that my body was completely limp; I was dead weight. So, he jerked his hands away, and I crumpled back on the bed. The jarring of my body brought me around somewhat, but I still could not move. I heard him begin to pace around the room. He was talking to himself. I was trying to understand what he was saying. *Why wasn't he calling 911? What was he waiting for?*

I concentrated as hard as I could to try to discern what he was saying. *Oh my God, he is actually practicing his speech on how to describe what happened. He is working on what he will say. Something about where he would live and how much he could get for my ranch.* I heard more muttering until a deep silence fell over me. Peace at last.

I was jarred awake by a sharp pain from knuckles of a strong hand digging into my breast bone with something sharp, something cold. The stranger continued to talk to me, asking me to stay with him. I heard several men's voices and hurried footsteps. I felt my body being jerked around. Something cold was jammed up my nostrils; sharp needles pierced my hand and arm. I was shoved inside a van with bright lights and I heard the doors slam shut. My body bounced with the rough ride of a utility vehicle as it raced away. I was so cold. I couldn't stop shivering; my neck was wrenched back with something jammed down my throat. The pain started to fade. My body stopped shivering.

A male voice yelled, "We are losing her! Give me the pads!"

EILEEN STEWART

Dancing with the Angels

I WAS FLOATING IN BLISSFUL NOTHINGNESS. No pain. No sadness. No tears.

And I saw Grandma, radiant and smiling. I sensed this overwhelming power of her love, which washed over me. Grandma was just a few feet away. I would say beyond my reach, but I didn't have a desire to reach out. It was enough to be near her. I felt a peace and contentment I had never experienced.

In an instant, I was pulled back. The pain. The cold. The jarring of the ambulance.

"We got her back!" I heard a deep voice yell.

Wait. I don't want to go back. Grandma! Grandma, take me with you.

I willed myself to go back; I didn't want them to save me. There was nothing left for me on earth but pain and betrayal.

"We're losing her again!" More voices. More jolts. A sudden halt. My body jerked around. Suddenly, all was quiet again.

Beside Grandma was Thomas, the love of my life. We had dated for several years and almost married. By choice, Tom remained single after I moved away. But I always came home for Christmas, and for thirteen years he had been invited to our holiday party. Tom quickly became one of the family and represented a time when I felt surrounded by the love of family.

Tom had passed away at the age of fifty-four just a few years earlier. He was a wonderful man with a zest for life and a tremendous sense of humor. Tom suffered immensely with juvenile diabetes but never complained or felt sorry for himself. By the time of his death, he had endured fourteen operations and several amputations. Tom dealt with his lot in life with dignity and grace. He was the perfect reminder of how to accept things as they are and to handle them in stride.

That incredible gift, that brief glimpse into what will someday be filled me with a new determination. I had no doubt when it was my time, that glorious place with my loved ones would be waiting. Whatever purpose I was put on this earth to do was yet to be done. But for now, I had to return to that great abyss of despair and with renewed resolve to somehow claw my way out.

January 21, 2007
Waking up in the Hospital

I OPENED MY EYES AND TRIED to bring my surroundings into focus.

"Where am I?" I asked groggily, and then realized there was no one there to answer. Nothing was familiar, but by the look of it, I was in a hospital. The furniture was sparse and the lights so bright. I closed my eyes again and fell back to sleep. The brush of a nurse's uniform woke me.

"Oh, you are finally awake. You're in the hospital," the nurse said matter-of-factly, "in a recovery room. Been here over a day and a half."

"Where's my husband?" I asked, looking around at the empty room with no sign of any visitors.

"Don't know, Ma'am," she said politely.

"Can I go home?" I asked.

"We're waiting on the doctor. Press that button if you need anything," she said over her shoulder as she left the room.

I rose slowly. I was a little dizzy. I opened the drawer beside me and dug my cell phone out of my purse.

"JB!" I said when he picked up the phone. "I'm awake. Can you come get me? I want to go home."

"No, I don't think so."

"No? What? Why not?"

"I'm kind of busy right now. I'll talk to you later."

Then I heard a click. In a state of disbelief, I pulled my phone from my ear to check the screen. Yep, he had hung up on me. I started calling my friends, but to my surprise, they turned me down one by one. They all said the same thing: JB had called them and instructed them not to give me a ride home. I tried to change their minds, but whatever reason he gave them must have been pretty convincing.

I finally reached Ben, a friend I hadn't talked to in many years. Ben said that JB had also called him. Ben and his wife had been my friends for so many years; he acquiesced and said they were on their way. They each stole glances at me sitting in the back seat of their van all alone, looking so vulnerable. I tried to conceal my shame, but my pitiable physical condition revealed the toll of the last few months. They took it all in—my shredded sweatshirt laced back together with surgical tape, my bare feet, and my gaunt, pale face. They had known me over seventeen years and they trusted me. They hadn't talked to me since I married JB; all they knew was that I needed help.

They respected that it was not a story I wanted to tell at the time, for which I was enormously grateful. I stepped out of the van and shut the door. I waved my thanks, and with a heavy sigh, I turned and walked up my front steps. It was pitch dark outside. There were very few lights on in the neighboring houses, so I assumed it was in the middle of the night.

I put the key in the lock, turned it, and with a slight hesitation, I stepped into the foyer. To my surprise, JB was sitting on the couch in the formal living room as if he just needed a place to sit and rest for a few minutes.

"What the hell are you doing here?" JB asked, eyes wide with surprise.

Actually, he almost sounded annoyed. It was after midnight but his face was red and he looked kind of sweaty. I shook my head; I didn't have the mental energy to worry about what he was up to.

I said over my shoulder, "Wow, nice greeting. Good to see you too," and shut the bedroom door.

Now I was home. I had to face what I had done. But that

could wait a few more hours. I crawled into my big empty bed and pulled my knees to my chest. Despite sleeping for almost two days, I was still exhausted and slipped quickly back to sleep.

January 22, 2007
Coming to Terms

I WOKE WITH A START. IT was as if my mind needed me to come to grips with what I had done. The harsh realization that I, once full of zest for life, had actually tried to end my life by my own hand.

I replayed my life over and over, examining the heights and the depths. What had propelled me to go to such an extreme? I was an intelligent woman; I loved life. I loved all God's creatures. I didn't believe in suicide. I would never want to take my own life, no matter what.

And yet, I did.

If there is one thing I knew how to control, it was my mind. I had always counted on my intelligence to rationalize any situation and to lead me out of any storm. Now, the very mind that I had counted on to keep me sane had told me to destroy myself. Without warning, it had morphed from friend to foe. What insanity would it tell me to do next? How do I ever trust myself again?

And then my mind filled with the vivid memory of my brief time "on the other side." A feeling of peace and warmth washed over me. It was going to be alright. It was abundantly clear it was not my time to die. I had taken over 100 Xanax and I weighed less than 105 pounds, yet I was still here. I had not fulfilled my purpose.

I guessed the first thing to face would be my failing marriage. I had tried to believe it was still viable, but I woke up alone the morning after trying to take my life. That pretty much summed it up.

I opened the door and strode towards the den. It was time to have the "talk" with JB. Things certainly weren't working. I walked around the corner and saw JB in his favorite recliner, the one I bought because he thought it was so comfortable. JB stared at the TV, evidently willing to avoid the situation.

I pulled on my boots and coveralls and headed out to the barn. At least the dogs and horses were glad I was still alive. It was a double-edged sword; part of me was grateful for their happiness to see me, and part of me worried if that would be all the love I would ever have. The feeling of melancholy was short-lived as I watched my geldings run around kicking up their heels, ears pinned back trying to inch the other one out of feed. I couldn't help but smile; they were such powerful and beautiful creatures. After I rubbed each of their noses, cleaned their hooves, and rubbed my hand over their muscles to make sure they were OK, I headed back to the house. My strides grew shorter as I reached the door.

As I expected, JB had vacated the den and was in the office on his computer. That was his haven that he had used for months to avoid me. But something had to change.

I knocked gently on the door frame and said, "I believe we have to talk. Would you please come into the den?"

I sat on the couch and waited for him to sit down. I reached for my glass of water and took a sip and cleared my throat. "Who was the girl that left a message on your phone?"

JB averted his eyes. "I know that must have sounded bad, but she is a very good friend."

I looked up at him and raised my eyebrow.

JB said, "She called me because her father was dying of cancer and so I provided support."

"Is that why you have become so distant? Because of her?"

"Yes, and I know it wasn't right. It was just for the weeks around Christmas."

"Wait, is this the one? The girl you lived with for several years in Alabama? Christy, I think."

"Yes. That was Christy."

Trying to keep my voice level, I said, "The message didn't sound like friends."

"Look, I have been getting close to her. It started innocently, but you have been so different. I guess I needed her, too."

I just dropped my head. There was enough blame to go around; neither of us had handled this situation well. A tear rolled down my cheek. I ordered myself not to cry.

I asked quietly, "So where does that leave us?

"It's totally different now. I can see what happened. The Xanax was the problem. You took the whole bottle, so you haven't taken it in a couple of days. I think that is what was affecting you that way. It was like you were an angry drunk. All of a sudden, your personality was totally different. But now, I see the girl I married. You are you again."

"I have to say, I do feel much more like myself. I was so agitated; I knew something was affecting my behavior but I couldn't stop it. It was so frustrating."

"Wait, that makes total sense. If you had a reverse reaction to it, and you thought it helped, you would take another one to calm you down. But it actually made the situation worse!"

"Oh, wow, that is probably it. I had such a hard time in Maryland. It was terrible. I wasn't myself, and everyone jumping on me just exacerbated the situation. Man, this is great. We figured out what was wrong." My jubilance quickly faded as I realized it didn't remove the chasm that had settled between us. I asked, "But what do we do about us?"

"Well, I had considered moving out, but this changes things. This is the first time in several weeks where I think I am talking to Audrey again, the girl I married."

"I don't want to throw in the towel." I stopped to wipe away the tears. "I have lost so much; you are all I have left." I cleared my throat and said in a stronger voice, "As long as it wasn't a full-blown affair, I can get past Christy. It is over, right? You are not going to keep calling her?"

"Of course not; that was just to help her while her father was so sick."

"Did he pass away?"

"Yes, he had cancer. So, at least he is at peace now."

"Well, I am willing if you are. And the first step is to be honest, and to start talking. Maybe we can somehow hit the reboot button on our marriage."

Several days passed by as we sheepishly worked our way around each other. We ate dinner together and watched the programs we used to watch. JB even started telling me about his work day again. Slowly, we were making our way back to each other. We had a reasonable weekend and even went out to a movie. We continued to carefully navigate conversation and did our best to reconnect. With each day, I gained a little bit of confidence that we might still have a chance.

FEBRUARY 3, 2007
JB WALKS OUT

SATURDAY MORNING, I WENT OUT into the den to join JB for a cup of coffee. JB looked up as I entered but averted his eyes quickly.

After carefully studying him, I asked, "What's wrong? You seem upset."

"I've found an apartment," JB said unceremoniously, "and I've signed a lease. I'm moving out."

I was stunned. I had been so busy watching my own life disintegrate before my eyes that I had completely missed how little feeling he had left for me. What was once such a passionate, romantic love had been replaced by contempt. When did he lose feeling for me entirely?

My head was spinning. Less than two weeks had passed since I had attempted suicide. When did he have any time to rent an apartment? How long had he been thinking about this?

I looked at him in disbelief. "What? We are starting to talk again. What happened between last weekend and this one? Is it her?"

"No," JB answered, "I told you that it wasn't a real affair. Christy has nothing to do with it. I just don't want to be married to you anymore."

"Where are you going to go?"

"Well, I signed a lease on an apartment," he repeated.

I stumbled over the words, "You what—signed a what—when?"

JB looked down at the floor. "Well, um, at lunch on Wednesday. I saw a sign when I drove by. They had some great move-in deal. Two hundred and fifty dollars off."

"What? You think it is time to end our marriage to save 250 dollars!"

"Well, maybe I moved too fast."

"Oh, can't you get out of it? Will you please try? We should try to work this out. If it was just Wednesday, I bet you can rescind the contract."

JB looked up. "You think so?"

"Yes, I do. Don't you think we deserve another chance?"

"I guess I could try and see if I can get out of the lease."

"Yes, please go right now and see what you can do." I went over and grabbed his keys and handed them to him.

JB walked to the door and said, "OK, I will be back soon. It is just right down the road."

I walked back to the couch and slowly sat down. I really couldn't believe that JB had actually gone out and signed a lease on an apartment. He was always tight with money, but to rush such a big move to save two hundred and fifty dollars? I lay on the couch, trying to control the tears and quiet the sobs. JB had to get out of the contract. This couldn't be over.

As the time passed, my mind couldn't let go of how odd this entire situation was. JB and I were actually talking; we hadn't done that in months. Why all of a sudden on a Wednesday would he decide that our marriage was over? He said he'd seen a sign for $250 off the first month's rent. I started to watch TV to pass the time; I was dying to know how it was going. I realized that an hour and a half had passed by and he wasn't back. The feeling that something was off continued to get stronger.

I remembered which folder he kept his phone bills in. There was something missing, something he wasn't telling me. Perhaps Christy was more than a friend. I sat at my large cherry desk JB liked to use to pay bills and let my fingers do the walking through the folders. My eyes settled on a folder without a label and I froze. It was a copy of the apartment lease; I gripped it with trembling fingers. I looked for the date, and there it was.

The lease was dated January 22, the first business day after I had attempted suicide!

These last ten days were just a charade. Oh my God, I am so stupid. I bought everything he said.

Now, I raced through the other folders looking for his cell phone bills. I spotted it and pulled the folder. I grabbed the stapled bills and scanned through each one. Wow. I counted ninety-three calls in December to his special "friend." I reviewed the next month and the one before that looking for when the affair started.

I couldn't believe my eyes. The daily calls to Alabama started back in August! I was such a fool!

The tears rolled down my face, but this time it was anger at myself for being so trusting.

Two and a half hours later, JB finally walked through the door. When he walked in, he saw the lease agreement and the phone bills on the coffee table. His eyes locked with mine. I decided I couldn't take him lying to my face anymore; it was easier just to let him know that I knew the truth.

I am not sure what I anticipated, a huge argument, or him crying and begging forgiveness, but he really didn't have any emotion. How could I be so blind not to comprehend that he didn't have any feelings left for me at all? I wondered if he'd ever cared about me. JB didn't even have the good grace to be embarrassed that he was caught in so many lies.

Now that the truth was out, he wasn't going to waste any more energy on the charade. JB calmly walked around the house pointing to things and telling me what personal property he was going to take.

"You don't have to remind me again; the ranch is yours," he said sharply. "But I am taking all the woodworking and photography equipment you bought me, the entertainment center, the new printer and computer. I am also taking the dining room table and chairs, and the china buffet," he continued. In essence, he was taking everything that was not nailed down.

I just sat there and watched him in astonishment. It was as if he were the lead actor on a Broadway stage and he had simply stepped into character. If it wasn't such a horrible situation, I probably would have commended his performance.

It was now so clear; JB didn't love me at all. My mind was suffused with fear. I didn't know if I could take care of myself. I was emaciated and my body racked with pain; I didn't even trust my own mind. But, my aunt's words kept echoing in my head: "Fight. Fight." I have no idea how, but I managed to stand up straight. I strode over to the hooks where we kept our keys. I grabbed the spare keys to his car and removed the house key from them. I tossed them to him.

I said with all the resolve I had left, "Get out; get out now!"

As I watched the door close behind him, I collapsed on the floor and broke into sobs. I had no idea what I was going to do now.

I couldn't believe this was happening. But then, I remembered that JB was the reason my family no longer spoke to me. He was the reason the doctor had stopped the antidepressants. What did it matter if he left? Wasn't I better alone than with someone I couldn't trust?

Then it hit me. I was not crying over the loss of JB; I was crying over the man JB had pretended to be. The man who just walked out the door, I'd never met.

FEBRUARY 4, 2007
THE ASSAULT

I N THE MORNING, I CALLED Mitch to remind him that he had said he would unload the shavings out of my truck. He answered the phone and said, "Sorry, Audrey, I can't this morning. I am playing golf. Afterwards, I have to help Laney get the house ready for the Super Bowl party."

I said, "OK. It doesn't have to be done today."

So the Super Bowl party is at their house this year.

I had seen them very little in the past few months. Actually, I hadn't been to their house since Thanksgiving. I doubted I would feel up to going this year. As I sat around the house, thinking about everything, I decided that going out for a couple of hours might do me good.

Laney's house was totally dark when I arrived for the annual Super Bowl party. *How strange.* I had just spoken with her husband this morning and he confirmed the party was at their house this year. But the room with the big-screen television was dark, and I didn't see any cars out front. None of their outside lights were on either. I had been to many parties at Laney's house; this was very odd. It was a large farm-type property, so maybe everyone was parked in the back.

Slowly, I drove around the back of the house, trying to be careful as they had been doing construction around the back. I saw the dark outline of a couple of vehicles, and noticed lights in the one room towards the back corner of the house. I parked and headed towards the back door.

When I opened the back door, I froze. Right in front of me was JB, drinking a beer. I was dumbfounded. JB had just moved out yesterday. *Was he over here telling them his side for that two hours when he pretended to try to cancel the new apartment lease?*

I thought Laney and Mitch were my friends—not his! We had been close for over ten years before JB even entered the picture. JB was the last person I expected to see! Yet there he was, grinning at me and gloating as if to say, "They are my friends now!"

I turned to leave, embarrassed and so disappointed. Mitch and Laney were two of the very few people I thought I could count on anymore, and now they were in his camp. As I passed JB's vehicle, I saw his phone on the console. I opened the door and grabbed it. By a stroke of luck, his dome light didn't come on when I opened the car door, so maybe they didn't see me take it. I just wanted to borrow it to delete my co-workers, my family, and my doctors' information, so JB would stop contacting them. I wanted those numbers out of his phone!

I got in my truck and hurried home. It was less than a mile, so it only took a few minutes. I parked my truck right next to the gate to block anyone from driving onto my property. It was several hundred feet from my front door, which somehow made me feel safer. While I was erasing numbers as fast as I could, I suddenly heard my dogs bark. Then I heard male voices and some truck doors slam. I looked out the window and saw several men walking around, talking heatedly amongst themselves and trying to figure a way onto my property. Thank God I had German Shepherds. The large barking dogs seemed to be enough deterrent to keep them from coming over the fence.

Fear gripped me as I watched through the window. They were very loud; they had probably been drinking for a while. I continued to watch them stumble around in the dark until they finally got back in their vehicle. They left my driveway with a chirp of the wheels.

I let out a long breath. My relief disappeared quickly as I realized they were only going back to the party to get drunker. I had no idea what JB had told them, but from the way Mitch and Laney had acted, it certainly wasn't in my favor. They would just come back. I needed to get the phone back to him, so they'd have no reason to come after me. It only took a few more minutes to delete my family's and doctors' numbers from JB's cell phone. As soon as I was finished, I climbed in my truck and drove back over to their house. Hopefully, I could slip JB's phone in the car, and then get out of there before they could get to me.

I was almost there when JB's cell phone lit up, startling me. I pulled over to look. It was a little love text from Christy, his mistress. I scrolled up and read through prior texts. They sounded like a couple of teenagers in heat. I was sick to my stomach. Here I was, just trying to survive, yet he was happy as a clam with his little girlfriend—the one he was trying to get pregnant.

I drove behind the house where JB's car was parked. I opened the door to his car and slipped the phone back in the exact place that I found it. Once again the dome light didn't go on. I found this odd, particularly since JB had recently purchased this late model, expensive sedan, which was in prime condition. At first, I thought that it was to my benefit, because there wouldn't be a flash of light to alert them that I was on the property. The absence of even one outside light or barn light illuminated made their parking area pitch black. Under these circumstances, a small dome light flashing on and off would be quite noticeable.

I looked up at the two thirty-inch windows of the little room where they were sitting before but did not see any suggestion that anyone was looking outside. I started to leave, but then stopped abruptly. I realized that retuning the phone did not solve my problem. Unless they knew I had returned the phone, the same group of intoxicated men was most likely going to come after me again. To compound the issue, JB's car was black with a black interior and his phone was black, making the chances of spotting the phone remote at best.

I let out a long breath. I didn't see any way out; I was going to have to walk back in and face the humiliation again to ensure they knew I had returned the phone. So, I retrieved the phone and walked carefully up the dark steps. When I reached the doorway, everyone was just staring at me. It was as if they were waiting for me. No one said a word. It was surreal.

I looked around the room to try to make sense of the situation. There was a small television on the coffee table, but no one seemed to be watching it. The room was small, not more than twelve by fifteen feet. Laney was in the corner right inside the door. JB was a few feet away in another chair and then Mitch and another man were seated towards the back of the room. The whole situation was so odd. None of the typical Super Bowl crowd was in evidence and the man in the back I had never seen before.

Now that I knew they clearly supported JB, I just wanted to get out of there. I turned to Laney and reached out with the phone.

"The guy you decided to side with is a cheat! But you probably already know that. Go ahead; take it, so I can get out of here," I pleaded.

Laney just sat there, motionless, with her hands jammed down between the cushions. I was sure they already knew he had a mistress, and furthermore, they didn't care. They were all in his camp. I was totally alone.

Laney continued to stare at me as I held out the phone, but she refused to reach up and take the phone. Laney was behaving so oddly. She had her infant on her lap, but she wasn't even holding her. Instead of encircling her child with her arms, she kept them against her sides jammed down into the part between the chair and cushions. I was dumbfounded by this. It didn't make any sense.

I didn't know what else to do, so I turned towards JB and took a step forward to be able to hand him his phone. Before I could take another step towards him, the stranger in the corner came barreling towards me. He was across the room in two long strides and his chest slammed against my face. My neck was fused, so I couldn't look up to see his face. I tossed the phone in JB's direction, hoping it would make the man stop.

Instead, he grabbed my arms and jerked me off the ground like a weightless toy. He flung me hard against the wall. My head crashed against the wall and pain shot down my neck. The man's fingers dug into my arms as he shook me like a rag doll. He slammed me into the wall again and again.

I was filled with fear and the feeling of helplessness as the beating continued. My head kept hitting the wall. Pain was shooting through my neck. My head was throbbing, and my knees buckled; I shook uncontrollably. I tried to speak but no words came. Thoughts of me in a wheelchair continued to race in my head.

"Stop! Please!" I yelled. "Stop! You will hurt my neck. I just had surgery. I am begging you; stop hurting me!" I couldn't process what was going on. Who was this guy? He was going to kill me. I caught glimpses of JB sitting in his chair. He wasn't even on his feet. He was actually smiling.

"Get off this property!" my attacker demanded as he shoved me into the wall yet another time. I stared in astonishment. "I am a cop! Are you ready to leave, or do you want to go to jail?"

I tried to pull his strong hands off my arms, but to no avail. He jerked me off the ground and tossed me out the door. My body slammed down hard on the deck. It was pitch black outside. I tried to pull myself up, but before I could get my feet under me, he shoved me hard. My body was propelled several feet and I slammed down on the wooden deck again. The wind knocked out of me, I tried desperately to pull air into my lungs. I was next jerked up in the air and tossed farther down the deck. I started to crawl, trying to get away. He grabbed me and tossed me down the stairs. I bounced down the stairs on my head and lay sprawled out on the ground.

I clawed at the ground in an attempt to pull my body towards my truck. Ignoring the stabbing pains and my throbbing head, I managed to pull myself up. I reached for the door handle of my truck. I clasped my hand around it with a fleeting hope of escape. I tried to open the door of my truck, but he viciously jerked my hand away and slammed me down on the ground, shoving his foot in my back. He ignored my screams and threatened once again to take me to jail. I lay there sobbing, pinned to the ground by his boot. He opened the truck door and stuffed me into the cab and slammed the door.

I was confused and couldn't process what to do next. My vision was blurry and my thoughts were scrambled, but I managed to get my trembling hands to put the key in the ignition. I started the truck and floored the gas pedal. I raced down their driveway as fast as I could. I glanced in the rearview mirror to make sure he wasn't following me and caught a glimpse of him standing there, laughing.

I drove into my driveway and jerked the truck to a stop. I sat there dazed, sobbing and shaking uncontrollably. For a few seconds, my mind cleared and I reached down and felt my legs. My heart filled with gratitude when I was able to pick up each foot and flex my ankles. I prayed that it meant the plates and screws had held in place. Maybe this attack didn't cause further injury to my spine.

My thoughts went fuzzy again. I sat there, afraid to move. Eventually, I opened the door of my truck and carefully stepped down. I staggered into the house and sat on the hall tree just inside the door. I felt my legs again and rotated each foot. My dogs rushed to me and then halted as if they sensed my fragile state. They gently licked my face and I hugged them for a long time. Moving carefully, I locked all the doors and headed to my recliner. I didn't turn on the TV for fear it would prevent me from detecting someone entering my property. Mind reeling, I sat in the dark in my recliner, both my hands gripping the baseball bat in my lap. The only sounds were garbled words of prayer as I pleaded to God to keep my assailant from coming after me.

My mind kept flashing back to the attack and I realized how strange it all was. I was being viciously beaten, yet they just sat watching. No one tried to help me. No one said one word.

And, what about JB? He was my husband. He didn't even bother to stand up, much less to defend me. I would never forget the eerie smile on his face as he casually took a sip from his beer.

I struggled to make sense of what had just taken place. Even in my confusion, I realized a police officer would not have brutally assaulted me. I knew strange things were happening, but he couldn't have been a cop. They just didn't do that.

I grabbed my cell phone and dialed Laney's number. Mitch answered the phone.

I said, "That guy said he was a cop. What is his badge number?"

The only answer I received was a click as he hung up the phone. I failed to notice the dust swirling up to the sky as the wagons circled.

EILEEN STEWART

FEBRUARY 4, 2007
EMERGENCY ROOM

LEEP WAS NOT POSSIBLE. I would finally drift off from exhaustion, only to wake up screaming and replaying the terrifying event. My neck was on fire, second only to my throbbing headache. I was certain it would become a migraine. I called my friend, Maggie, to tell her what happened. I needed to hear a friendly voice. I was not thinking clearly, and I was having great difficulty recounting the story.

Maggie told me I was slurring my words and advised me to go to the emergency room right away. She said she thought I had a concussion. I was confused, but that sounded like good advice. I locked the dogs inside and drove my car outside the gate. I then parked my truck on the inside of the gate to block access to my property.

I got back in my car but forgot where I was going. I looked at my cell phone screen and read the last call out was to Maggie. That reminded me I was supposed to go to the hospital. I reached for the dash and typed hospital in the navigation unit. The mechanical voice said to get on a road. I wasn't sure what road it meant, so I drove to the nearest highway. I continued to make turns but none of them corresponded to the map illuminated on my dash.

I took a left, and then another left. But no matter how many turns I made, I wound up back to where I started. So, I tried again. I made a right and another right, but I was back to the same place. My vision was blurry, so I continued to blink my eyes in an effort to read the display. The voice repeatedly told me to find a safe place to make a U-turn. I could see the outline of the hospital but couldn't find the entrance.

I dialed Maggie again.

Maggie said, "What did the doctor say? I was starting to worry."

"I haven't gotten to the hospital yet. I can't figure it out. I see the building but the map doesn't show the roads right."

"Audrey, it has been two hours. It is almost midnight. You have been driving all this time?"

"Um, yeah, it has been a while. I lost track of the time."

Maggie stayed on the phone with me and managed to direct me into the ER parking lot. I entered through the sliding doors and shielded my eyes as the bright lights cranked my migraine up a notch. My head felt like there was an axe splitting it in two. My neck was on fire. They nurse handed me a clipboard with forms on it. I stumbled back to the row of seats and tried to fill out the forms. I struggled with the most basic questions. It took all my concentration to fill out my name and address. I lay down across three plastic chairs with my arm shielding my eyes from the harsh lights.

I called Dee to tell her what happened.

"What's going on, Audrey?" said Dee. "Your speech is all slurred. Have you been drinking?"

"What? No. I mean, I was attacked. It is such a crazy story. I don't know where to start. This guy beat me to a pulp; I am so worried about the plates and screws."

Dee interrupted again and said, "Where are you?"

"I am at the emergency room. I was at Laney's house; you know, the Super Bowl party. Anyway, this big guy, I have never seen him before—"

Dee interrupted me again. "Where is your truck?"

"What? My truck? Well, it is at the front gate, huh?" I said curiously.

"Audrey, can a vehicle get in?"

Even with a concussion, this seemed like an odd question to me. I willed myself to think, to make sense of this through my hazy thoughts.

"No, only a person to feed the animals. My belongings are safe. Why?"

"Where are the keys?" Dee asked.

That question got my attention. Something was wrong. I had just told her I was assaulted and in the emergency room. Yet her main concern was if a vehicle could get on my property. Come to think of it, Dee didn't seem surprised to hear that I had been attacked.

I tried desperately to make sense of the situation and why she would ask such a question. Then, it hit me. *Oh my God, she is helping JB clear out the place.*

I needed medical attention, but I couldn't leave my animals and property unattended. JB had already drained the bank account. I couldn't afford to lose what little I had left. I heard the bang of the clipboard hit the floor as I stiffly made my way out through the sliding doors. My battered body was fueled by adrenaline as I agonizingly staggered towards my car.

EILEEN STEWART

ALL-CONSUMING FEAR

I REACHED THE HOUSE AND MY truck was still in the driveway. I said a silent prayer of thanks. I limped up the steps and unlocked the front door. My dogs ran to me, tails wagging happily. I quickly sat down; I was so weak they could easily knock me over with their jubilance. I sat there and petted them with trembling hands as tears ran down my face. At least I still had them. They would keep me safe.

I took a very long, hot shower, trying to loosen up the muscles. Unfortunately, I was all too familiar with how I was going to feel in the morning. I finally got out of the shower and carefully blotted myself dry. I looked in the mirror and saw my swollen eyes and the numerous marks from his strong fingers already turning to bruises.

I slowly climbed into bed and tried to fall asleep. I was exhausted. I finally dozed off, but then I jerked awake. My dogs ran into the room and stared up at me. Then I realized I was still screaming. I watched TV for a while in an effort to clear my mind. Every time I dozed off, I relived the beating—the stranger's fingers biting into my arms, my head hitting the wall, the pain shooting through my neck.

I wish I had seen his face. How would I even know him if I passed him in the grocery store?

All I knew was that he was tall. But he was on top of me in two large strides across the small room. I didn't even look at him until he grabbed me, but with the plates in my neck, I couldn't look up to see his face. How was I going to protect myself against a man I couldn't recognize?

I continued to try to fall asleep, but the result was the same. I would wake up screaming, begging the man to stop hurting me. I was so exhausted; I was in so much pain, but the fear kept me awake. Even though most of my property remained, JB had already done irreparable damage. He had betrayed me in every possible way. JB had taken all my money, had an affair, estranged me from my friends and family, and abandoned me after a suicide attempt. But that was nothing in comparison to what he had stripped me of now: my peace of mind. I lay there and wept and prayed.

Please God, just let me fall asleep for a little while.

February 5, 2007
Assault and Battery Complaint

THE NEXT MORNING, I WAS jarred awake by the ringing of my cell phone. Pain shot through my shoulder and neck as I reached for the phone. I turned it to see the screen and Maggie's picture lit up. I would have to call her back. I slowly got up and hobbled to the bathroom. Every muscle complained; I felt as if I had been hit by a truck. I stole a quick glance in the mirror; I looked awful. I took a very long, hot shower, but it gave me little relief.

I gingerly touched my body with the towel to dry myself. I heard the notification of a text from my phone. I grabbed it from the counter and looked at the screen. It was a text from Maggie:

I still can't believe you were attacked last night! My husband said you should file a police report right away. I know you must be in terrible pain, but please do that today. If you can't drive yourself, call me.

I knew she was right, but it brought tears to my eyes to think about moving that much. I had to pick up some horse feed anyway; I wouldn't let them go hungry. I could have asked a neighbor to help, but my animals were the only thing holding me together. Taking care of them was the only shred of normal left in my life, and it was my lifeline. After the feed store, I went over to the sheriff's office. Despite the agony, I managed to fill out a complaint for assault and battery. I wasn't sure what would be done, but at least I had started the process. It did make me feel slightly better.

I was so happy to arrive back home where I could lay down. I grabbed the big ice packs and positioned them under my shoulders and neck. I tried futilely throughout the day to control the pain. I heard another text notification. It was probably Maggie checking on me.

I read Maggie's text: *How are you? Did you file a report?*

I struggled to type a text back. It read: *Yeah--laid out with migraine--later.*

She knew not to contact me back when I had one of my debilitating migraines. I laid back down and tried to force myself to sleep without success. The minute I closed my eyes, I could feel those fingers digging into my arms and the flashes of pain when my head slammed against the wall. So, I just lay there and prayed for the nightmare to end.

FEBRUARY 6, 2007
SERVED

I WAS IN SO MUCH PAIN when I fed the horses that I decided to call the office of the surgeon who had performed the third spinal surgery. I wanted an x-ray to verify that the plates and screws had not been displaced during the attack. During the long drive downtown, I was consumed with the fear that they may have to operate again to fix this latest damage.

I couldn't imagine surviving another spinal surgery. I recounted enough of the incident to convince him to send me towards the door marked X-ray. He asked me if I had filed a police report for the attack. Given his perplexed expression, I was glad I could answer yes to his question. After he stared at me for another minute, he left the room. I felt so frail, all alone perched on that little table suffused with fear of what the x-ray might mean.

What was taking so long? Please God, not another surgery.

Finally, the surgeon entered the room with a grey film in his hand. He walked over, slipped it up under the clip on the viewer, and flipped on the light. At this point, I had seen so many x-rays that even I could see the hardware was still intact. My eyes filled with tears of joy as I slowly made my way back to my car.

Thank God!

As I drove myself home, I gave thanks to God that this attack did not paralyze me and did not require another surgery. Either event could have easily happened given my fragile state. I was in extreme pain and it would take me weeks to recover from these recent injuries, but I would heal.

I felt a little better knowing that this was all soft tissue damage and my spine was OK. I certainly knew how to treat it. Ice and rest, more ice and more rest.

Maybe I can sleep now.

I went to the bedroom to lay down for a nap. I was so exhausted. I had been awake for close to forty hours and I had to get some sleep. But again, each time I started to fall asleep, I woke up screaming and covered in sweat. This happened over and over.

My mind became cloudier and cloudier. *Did that really happen?*

I lost track of time. I continually fell asleep and then woke with a start in a pool of sweat. I relived the attack over and over. I tried to watch TV to take my mind off of the attack.

Suddenly, there was a banging on the door.

Oh my God! Who was that?

Was it the stranger coming back to finish the job he had started?

Oh no, please God, no.

I was exhausted but the adrenaline shot through me and I was wide awake. I grabbed my .38 from its hiding place under the coffee table. Even with the pistol in my shaking hand, I felt utterly defenseless. I held it down against my thigh as I slowly and fearfully approached the door.

I yelled through the door, "Go away!"

A man's voice said with frustration, "Open the door. I have papers for you."

"I don't know who you are. Get off my property!" I yelled fearlessly, while the panic welled inside me.

My male German Shepherd was by my side. Gunther was over 100 pounds so I reached out and put my hand on his back. I leaned on my hand to steady myself.

The voice yelled, "I need you to open the door. I am not leaving!"

Oh, my God! Who is this? Had he come to hurt me? Is he a friend of the assailant or my husband?

My house was a ranch, therefore it didn't have an elaborate front entrance. The front door was a simple steel door without a peephole or glass pane in the center. It didn't even have any side windows, so there was no way for me to know who it was. I wasn't opening the door for anything.

I yelled as my voice cracked, "Go to the back door where there is glass so I can see you."

I went to the back door with my little .38 pistol, careful to keep Gunther close to my side. I ducked around the corner where I could see his face through the window. I could see the man's face through the glass, and by its position in the frame, I could tell the man was short. I creeped slowly along the wall until I was near the door knob. He still couldn't see me from where I stood.

Given his size, I was certain it was not my assailant but I couldn't understand what he was doing at my house. Could he be a friend of the assailant, or another friend of JB's? I lived way out in the country; nobody just stopped by. For the third time, he yelled my name.

In the most assertive voice I could muster, I said, "Get off my property now."

This time he said with anger, "Look, I did what you said. Now, come out here and sign this. I am not leaving until you do!"

I slowly raised the gun to his eye level. His eyes grew wide in disbelief. He was now staring directly down the barrel of my .38-caliber pistol. He immediately dropped the folded document and ran for his vehicle. I turned around, leaned against the door, and slowly slid down to the floor. I was out of breath; my heart pounded as the tears rolled down my face.

I am OK. He is gone now. I am safe.

I sat there, staring into space for a long time, holding the gun to my chest, thanking God the man didn't get inside.

I finally stood and opened the door. I took two steps out on the porch and quickly grabbed the document which he had dropped on the deck. As soon as the document was in my hand, I jumped back in my house, slammed the door, and turned the lock. My heart was racing again.

After I calmed back down, I opened the document. It looked official. As I read the first few lines, I couldn't believe my eyes. I read it again. It was a petition for divorce filed by my husband that very morning. And then I looked at the last paper. Wow. As if the divorce petition wasn't enough, there was a court-issued temporary restraining order filed by my husband!

A restraining order? A judge actually granted JB an order of protection against me? I was the one assaulted. The man who beat me claimed to be a police officer. I didn't believe it because of his actions. But, what if he was?

I was taught from a very young age that if I was frightened, all I had to do was call for the police and they would come to my rescue without hesitation. I was taught that they were noble and existed for only one purpose: to safeguard me at all cost and punish anyone who hurt me.

But, what do you do when the "protectors" become tormentors?

I no longer had confidence that, if I dialed 911, there would be someone racing to help me. The very person I needed protection from wore the exact same uniform that was supposed to protect me. The sight of a badge or even a glimpse of a passing squad car no longer comforted me. Instead, it produced panic and fear.

Everything I had ever thought was being challenged. I thought I had a good career but now it was gone. I thought I had a marriage and it was gone. Now I had been brutally beaten and yet I was the one who had a restraining order against me.

My family and friends had been turned against me. My husband had set me up. JB had completely destroyed my trust in people. I would forever see strangers in a different light. I came to the horrible realization that I no longer had anyone to turn to, no one to trust, and any confidence I had ever possessed in anyone to protect me was gone.

The world as I knew it no longer existed.

EILEEN STEWART

February 8, 2007
First Divorce Hearing

I WOKE VERY EARLY, BUT AT least I had managed a couple hours of sleep. Despite the time, I decided to get up anyway. I wouldn't be able to go back to sleep and it would take me a long time to get ready for court. I swung my legs over the bed as sharp pains shot through my back and up through my neck.

Oh, wow. I am even stiffer than I was yesterday. I didn't think that was possible.

I put on my coveralls and went out to feed the horses with the dogs trotting happily at my side. When I got back to the house, I took a long, hot shower and dutifully dressed in a suit for my divorce court hearing. I was still dumbfounded that JB had filed for divorce at all. The last two weeks he had made me feel as if he wanted to work through it. Yet, he filed for divorce the day after I filed the complaint against my attacker at the "supposed" party. And to add insult to injury, JB had filed for a temporary restraining order that same day. The temporary is usually granted until the formal hearing where the judge hears from both sides. I looked at the bottom of the paper which noted it was scheduled for February the twentieth. So, I would just have to deal with it for two weeks and then I would have a chance to tell my side.

The TRO was most certainly in retaliation for my assault and battery complaint. A restraining order against me filed two days after I was attacked seemed ludicrous when I first read it. But after careful consideration, it was strategic move. It would probably go a long way to discredit me and perhaps help protect Laney and Mitch from any civil action I could bring regarding the injuries sustained in their house. *Hell, if JB would apply his efforts for good instead of evil, he could probably find a cure for cancer!*

I managed to drive up to the courthouse and sit through the hearing. I was completely unprepared. Given JB's performance over the last two weeks, I hadn't contacted any divorce attorneys, much less retained one. I was so blindsided by the whole mess that JB had the clear advantage. Due to sleep deprivation, I was barely coherent, and the pain was so excruciating that I found it difficult to concentrate. Any representation would have really helped, but I did the best I could. Basically the court would decide what property we would each get at a later date. The marriage was certainly over, now it was just math.

I pulled in the driveway and put the car in park while I expelled a very long breath. I slowly got out of my car and climbed up the steps. I walked in and was greeted by my dogs; they always lifted my spirits. I held the door open so they could go out and eat their breakfast. I free fed them with a large pet feeder that was in the alcove by the front door. They didn't have a chance to eat before I left for court, so they were probably hungry. Annie was Gunther's mother so she always ate first.

I carefully peeled off my suit. I put on some jeans and a comfortable shirt and headed out to the den to watch television. I must have drifted off for a while from sheer exhaustion. When I opened my eyes, I realized my dogs were still outside. I stood and hurried to the front door. Annie was laying a few feet away from the feeder. Something was off; she barely lifted her head when I opened the door. I sat down on the deck and petted her. I lifted up her head. She tried to stand, but as she did, she started throwing up.

Oh my God!

Ignoring my protesting muscles, I somehow managed to help Annie into the back seat of my truck. I was about to get in the driver's seat and I stopped. I turned back and looked at the feeder on the deck. I ran back and picked it up and put it on top of the picnic table, out of Gunther's reach. I drove like a maniac to get her to the vet.

I was too weak to get her out of the truck and had the office staff come out to get her. In halted sobs I begged my veterinarian to save her life. I told him to treat her for poisoning. The vet just looked at me incredulously. I pleaded, "You have been my vet for fifteen years, just treat her for poisoning." Then I collapsed on the floor. The office staff helped me over to a seat.

After examining Annie, the veterinarian asked to keep her overnight. They needed to run something through her to filter her blood. That was fine with me—at least she was safe and it looked like she would be OK.

As I thought about it on the way home, it became more and more clear to me: this man would not stop. If I pressed assault charges, he was going to kill my animals—simple as that. Now, my animals, the one thing that was OK in my life and gave me some comfort, were in mortal danger. Everything that gave me peace of mind had been stripped away.

As soon as I got home, I removed the dog feeder and threw all the dog food away.

But what could I do? I had no idea who attacked me.

Wait, Laney knows who he is. My only chance to stop him was through Laney.

I picked up the phone and dialed Laney. I assumed she would not pick up, so I left this message: "Laney, I guess you thought that was funny the other night. Well, you can do whatever you want to me, but leave my animals alone. If one of my animals dies, I will hunt you down like the dog you are."

It was all I could think to do. Maybe it would scare Laney enough to tell my attacker to stop hurting my animals. I was in a world of hurt but I couldn't survive one of my animals being killed or hurt because of me. What kind of person was this who would attack a hundred-pound post-surgical patient or a helpless animal?

Once again, I crawled into my bed and tried to force myself to sleep. Annie was safe but I still couldn't rest. I needed to think of something else to protect them, in case my phone call didn't prompt Laney to call the evil bastard off.

I had two outside entrances and I needed my .38 at my bedside table, so I went to the gun store and purchased two more guns: a Bersa 9mm and a Glock 9mm pistol. I loaded them and hid them at each door's entrance. From that point on, I answered the door with a pistol at my side. And every time I ventured outside to take care of my animals, I carried a pistol with me.

Now that I had a weapon at every door, perhaps I could get a little more sleep. I lay on the couch watching TV, trying desperately to distract myself from the horrible recurring images of the assault: the feeling of my head hitting the wall over and over again, the unbelievable feeling of helplessness as those powerful hands clawed at me and bit into my arms, repeatedly slinging me against a wall. I prayed for sleep, but any relief was sparse. The token few hours of rest were the result of sheer exhaustion.

FEBRUARY 20, 2007
THE PRIVATE INVESTIGATOR

I WEARILY RETURNED FROM THE SECOND divorce hearing. I couldn't believe on top of all the physical pain, I had to deal with the emotional pain of a divorce. I owned the house before we met. I made more money. I paid more than JB did for bills, plus I paid for any horse-related activities. JB had a mistress for months and he certainly didn't care if I lived or died.

Why couldn't he just go away and leave me alone?

I went inside and changed out of the suit I had worn for court and grabbed a pair of jeans. I pulled them up and was amazed that I could grab the waist and ball it up in a fist. These used to be my tightest pair of jeans.

Two years of liquid diet sure will slim you down.

I went out on the deck and waited for the private investigator I had contacted over the weekend. I found him through an internet search. I wanted him to probe into JB's background. I wanted to know exactly what happened with JB's first marriage. From the snippets JB had relayed to me, my situation was eerily similar to his first divorce. Something deep in my gut told me there was much more going on than I was aware of. I wanted to be armed with this information in divorce court. JB was clearly not "going quietly into that good night."

Little things were starting to stand out in my mind. The behavior of Dee, for instance, really astounded me. She came over after I called her crying the day JB left. I remembered it vividly, perhaps because it was so out of character. Dee's look of incredulity, and her callous statement: "Are you really surprised,

Audrey?" I didn't know how to answer. I had just told her I was getting yet another migraine and that I had to go lay down.

I wanted answers. No, I needed answers.

My father, who had always been somewhat chauvinistic, was certainly convinced the failing marriage was entirely my fault. I was now aware JB had been filling his head with lies, but there had to be a way to prove it to my father. I prayed this investigator would find some information that could make sense of all this. This investigator was my last hope. Everything hinged on him demonstrating that this was JB's pattern.

I saw a car come down the road; it slowed and turned in my gate. It pulled in very slowly and I started to worry. Something seemed off. It was a dark-colored Crown Vic with cheap hubcaps, the type of vehicle they always used for undercover police work.

A fortyish type of woman stepped out and said, "I am Connie, Steve's assistant."

She walked casually over to the picnic table and sat down. She immediately started fooling with her phone.

My eyes darted back and forth between her and the man in the mysterious car. I looked at the car and said, "Hey, would you please get out of the car?"

The man didn't seem to hear me. He was looking down at something and was distracted.

My mind was filling with fear. I reached under the magazine I had on the table and slowly pulled out my Glock. I looked at the girl and said, "Hey, please tell him to get out of the car and show me his hands. I've had some trouble here."

She flicked a quick look at me and saw what was in my hand. With wide eyes, she said nervously, "Steve, hey! Come on out. Like now!"

Hearing the anxiety in her voice, Steve quickly understood the gravity of the situation. He immediately opened the door and said, "OK, here I am. Sorry, I was finishing a report."

Steve furtively glanced at the 9mm I had set back on the picnic table. His experience with volatile situations was readily apparent by how well he handled the current circumstances.

Steve looked directly into my eyes and said, "OK, clearly you have had some trouble." He spread his hands open and directed us to the picnic table. He said, "Why don't we all just take a breath and sit down; you can tell me about it?"

Steve casually glanced at the pistol on its side, the grip still loosely encircled by my hand. He sat down gingerly and put his hands flat on the table, "And if it is all the same to you, how about you move your hand a little farther away from that Glock."

With an imperceptible head nod, I carefully moved my hand several inches away from the gun. I watched his assistant with my peripheral vision and never broke eye contact with Steve.

I took a deep breath and launched into the unbelievable chain of events. I began: "OK, this is going to sound crazy. I mean I am an intelligent accomplished person; this kind of stuff simply doesn't happen to people like me."

As I searched for the right words, I watched his eyes taking in the surroundings: a beautiful custom barn, a 1,200-square-foot shop, the freshly painted large ranch house. All the buildings were color coordinated and the property was clearly well kept. A nice, clean crew-cab diesel was hooked up to an expensive three-horse aluminum trailer and a sleek little import sat in the driveway.

His eyes scanned over me once again, detecting how incongruous my physical condition was to my surroundings: the lackluster hair that fell loosely around my pale, gaunt face, the circles under my eyes that exposed the sleep deprivation. My baggy jeans hung loosely on my small, emaciated frame. I slowly and carefully took a seat across from him. His eyes followed my halting movements as my expression revealed the pain.

There was no easy way to explain my situation, so I decided to start with his perspective. I said, "Look around; you can see I have a nice place. Well, it has taken me over twenty years to build this place and I had it long before I met my husband."

Steve's eyes scanned the place again and he looked at me with a new-found respect.

"I won't drag you through the minutia, but I had a car accident and sustained serious injuries which necessitated several surgeries. However, that was not actually the difficult part." I noted Steve's eyebrow raised and he tilted his head. "Apparently my 'beloved' took advantage of the situation and has been talking to my doctors and my family to a point that nothing I say is believed. I am taking a myriad of prescriptions and I'm not even sure why my doctor prescribed them."

I could see I was losing him, so I decided to leave the medication out of the story. "From the little bit that JB has told me about his first divorce there are some striking similarities. They were married Catholic and at some point she had a nervous breakdown. JB moved her to Georgia and apparently her brothers came down from New York to take her home. They told her to take what she absolutely needed and they were on their way. I believe he even said that her family never allowed him to see her again."

"This didn't—well, you know—concern you at all?"

"Well, my mother was bipolar and I think he was trying to show how caring and understanding he is. Believe it or not, the way he presented it, it actually made him look good. But with what I know now, it boils down to what I just said. Without all the spin."

I continued, "My real problems started when I was brutally assaulted at a neighbor's house. I was seriously injured but had to leave the ER without treatment when it became apparent that JB was checking to see how he could gain access to the property."

Seeing his confusion, I said, "Again, it is a very complicated story. I only need to know what happened in his first marriage. JB has already helped himself to any monies he could access or anything expensive he could remove quietly. Basically, I want the hemorrhaging to stop and I want to be damn sure I keep my ranch!"

I looked around at my ranch as a tear rolled down my face. I quickly bit my bottom lip to stop it from trembling.

Steve politely listened but had trouble keeping the skepticism out of his expression. He cleared his throat and picked up the pen on his legal pad to capture the pertinent details.

"So," Steve asked, "how long ago did you file for divorce?"

"Actually, he filed for divorce. It was a total surprise to me; the papers were dropped on my back porch with a TRO. The timeline is this: I was assaulted on the fourth, filed assault and battery charges on the fifth, and JB filed for divorce and a TRO on the sixth. My first divorce hearing was the eighth." As he was taking notes, I said quickly, "Actually, I don't care about stuff. My immediate concern is to protect my animals."

"I don't understand. I thought you said you were attacked."

"Yes, I was, but the day I had to appear in divorce court someone put something in the dog food. After my female Shepherd ate the food that morning, she started throwing up. I rushed her to the vet and told them to treat her as if she was poisoned, which they did, and she is OK now."

"How do you know it happened then, exactly? When you were in divorce court?"

"Well, I am on disability and I don't ever leave the house."

"Never?"

"Well, I used to go to the store or run an errand occasionally. But ever since the night I was assaulted, I don't leave the house at all. I have friends who actually go shopping for me. I never leave the dogs unattended. If they are outside, they are with me. Otherwise, they are locked in the house. Unfortunately, the container that held the dog kibble was on the porch. As a matter of fact, I returned from the second hearing about an hour ago, but the feeder is inside now."

Steve looked around and asked, "You said dogs; I only see one?"

My head whipped around, but I didn't see my Annie. I was so distressed about him coming in the driveway and not getting out of the car, that I hadn't paid attention to both of them. Both Steve and I looked at Gunther, my large male German Shepherd. Gunther slowly rose, but was very shaky on his feet.

I jumped up and ran up the stairs towards the house.

Steve stood and walked up to the large green bucket of water a few feet away from the picnic table. I came running out, but stopped abruptly when I saw him standing at the water bucket. Steve read the panic on my face and looked down at the water.

"There is an oily residue on the top of this water," Steve said, leaning until he was close enough to smell the water. His expression turned very serious. "It smells like paint thinner."

Steve immediately dumped the water on the ground. He hastily asked me if they have any other water source outside.

My eyes fill with tears as I screamed, "No. Oh, my God! Not again!"

I went running into the house to find Annie. Steve followed me into the house. He watched as I ran over to my female dog. She was just lying there very still. I dropped to the floor and gently lifted her head to see the glassy stare.

My heart sank. How long did they have access to the water after I came back? How much would they have ingested?

I said, "I am sorry; I will call you later. I need to get them to the vet now!"

Steve was not sure what to do, but he slowly started walking out the door. After a few steps he stopped. He turned around and said, "Make sure you call the police and report this. This can help you in the divorce."

I waved my hand over my shoulder so he would know I heard him. I heard the two car doors close and the gravel under the tires as the car slowly drove out towards the gate.

I frantically dialed 911 and asked for the detective that gave me his card when I filed the assault and battery complaint. He wasn't available, so I told them just to note that my animals had been attacked a second time. I needed to go; I needed to try to save my dogs.

I was desperate to get them medical help, but I couldn't even get Annie to get on her feet. I tried everything to coax her, but she didn't have the strength. Annie was the smaller of the two and she weighed ninety-five pounds. Given my weakened state, there was no way for me to load either of them in the truck alone.

Oh, my God, I can't let them die!

EILEEN STEWART

FEBRUARY 20, 2007
THE ARREST

I SAT ON THE FLOOR BESIDE Annie, tears rolling down my cheeks. I had my phone in my hand and I was rifling through numbers, trying to find someone who could help me and would be available in the middle of the afternoon. I left several messages but no one answered.

The sudden rapping on my door startled me. Annie and Gunther would normally have warned me that someone had arrived on the ranch, but they did not react.

Instead of a friendly knock, a deep male voice called my name and pounded on the door.

Fear ripped through my body as I grabbed the 9mm pistol—just in case. I couldn't make out what he was saying. Bewildered, I wondered if it is the police coming to help me. *Or, is it someone else?*

Painfully, I raised myself from the couch and hobbled across the living room towards the front door. I jumped as the deep male voice yelled again and I heard more pounding on the door.

He was at the front door. I once again cursed the blind entrance. The front door didn't have glass, side windows or even a peep-hole. The door was located in the nook of the deck which was not visible from any window in the house. I had absolutely no idea who was on the other side of that door.

Actually, it didn't matter. I wouldn't have known if it was the assailant. He was on top of me so fast that I never saw his face.

"Coming!" I yelled, as I grappled with the lock and awkwardly tried to open the latch with trembling hands. Cautiously, I opened the door, while holding my gun behind my hip, out of sight.

Towering before me in a brown uniform was a tall, muscular man with a stern expression. He looked ready to spring into action. Looking back on the attack, I dismissed the attacker claiming to be a cop, but what if he was? This man at my door was extremely tall—it was the only thing I knew about my attacker. And this guy who was staring me down was a mountain of a man!

Oh, my God! What if my attacker really was a cop as he claimed and he is here to finish the job he started?

Thoughts raced through my mind. I tried to keep them straight. But, like the night of my attack, something was off. I couldn't make sense of it. Why was there just one officer instead of two? What if he didn't want a witness? If he was responding to my call to help me, he should be kind, but this man was angry.

His eyes focused on something behind me. I turned and saw my Gunther walking to my side, but he was unsteady on his feet. I moved the gun from behind my leg out to the side, fearing Gunther would bump it and it could go off. The officer grabbed his gun from his holster and trained it on Gunther.

"No!"

The wave of my hand caught the officer's attention and he noticed the Glock in my hand. In a flash, he turned his weapon away from Gunther and pointed it at my forehead.

"Put the gun down!"

I was stunned.

Do I drop my weapon and risk being killed? Or, do I kill him in fear for my life?

For what seemed like an eternity, I stared down the barrel of his pistol, caught in a deadly dilemma.

"Drop the weapon!" he yelled, his hand trembling.

Our eyes locked on each other with intensity.

"Please don't kill me!"

Instantly, he was over the threshold and was spinning me around, slamming me against the wall. He didn't have a clue how fragile I was, held together by a plates and screws. Tears rolled down my cheeks as the cold steel bit into my wrists.

Thoughts of another beating raced through my mind. I stood there, shoulders drooped and head down. In my mind, it was over; they had won, and my attacker had me now. No witnesses, he could simply shoot my dogs. I stood there motionless and waited for the physical abuse I was surely about to endure.

I quietly mumbled, "Please make it quick."

"You are under arrest . . . ."

I was too stunned to hear the rest. All I could think about was my dogs.

The officer recovered his wits and started to listen to my babbling. I begged him to get medical attention for my poisoned dogs.

I said, "You can take me anywhere you want, but please, please, get help for my dogs."

He turned and looked over at Annie, who was laying in the exact position as she had been before he knocked on the door.

I tried to explain everything, but it didn't even make sense to me. But, my dogs' behavior was consistent with my story. A normal German Shepherd would have torn him to pieces if he had rushed into the house and attacked its owner.

The officer looked over at Annie and said, "That one over there didn't even lift her head?" He then looked at Gunther who had fallen down near the door. There was drool coming from his muzzle and his glassy eyes stared at space.

"Yes, I know. I am begging you. Can we please wait for animal control to take them to get them medical help? And, then take me to jail or whatever." I looked up at him with tears in my eyes, "I am begging you. Please don't let them die."

I was now sobbing uncontrollably. At that point, his puzzled look was replaced by compassion. He realized neither I nor my dogs were a threat to anyone in our current condition. I silently thanked God as he turned his head and depressed the button on the radio and called for Animal Control.

The white truck arrived. The dogs were loaded, and the truck took off. I prayed to God to save my precious animals! I didn't care about myself right now. I was so relieved they would get medical treatment and be taken care of. They were innocent victims caught up in the melodrama of a marriage gone awry.

The officer climbed into the front seat of the police car, put the key in the ignition and the car started moving. I gritted through the pain to turn my neck around to take a last look at my ranch. It was part of me. I wondered if I would ever see it again.

Felons with Wings

THERE WERE SEVERAL WOMEN ALREADY in the holding cell when the officer shoved me in and slammed the steel door shut. I heard the turn of the lock and the sound seemed to echo forever. All eyes were on me as I stood there, frozen. A couple of them whispered and bumped elbows. It was a motley group; most of them were dressed provocatively with tattoos, some plainly dressed like anyone you see in the store. I don't know what I expected, but there were all shapes and sizes, the look of desperation was all they shared.

A young girl with dark hair said, "You just as well better sit down, hon'; you could have a long wait."

The girl on the other bench said, "I don't know, girlfriend; she looks like she ain't done nothing wrong in her whole life. I bet she be outta here this afternoon."

The officer came in and pointed to me. "You. You get a phone call."

He led me over to a bench where I sat and waited to use the pay phone. The wall was covered with tattered advertisements for bail bondsmen. I scanned them offhandedly while I waited my turn. This world was so unfamiliar to me.

I couldn't wait to call my dad. I felt sure once he knew my situation, he would leap to my defense. He was not only an attorney; he was a judge! He would be outraged when he heard what happened. Finally, it was my turn. I heard the phone ringing.

"Dad?" I said excitedly. "I need your help!"

"Where are you?" he asked. I was taken aback by his harsh tone.

"I'm in jail, Dad. I need you to get me out of here!"

"Yes, eh, well. JB told us you tried to kill a cop."

"What? When did you talk to JB? Never mind, this is all a misunderstanding. I have no idea why I was arrested. They came to my home. My residence, Dad! Gunther ran to the door, I moved the gun so he wouldn't hit it. I just was moving it out of the way!"

"Well," he said, raising his voice, "that sounds pretty much like you raised a gun at an officer. What the hell were you thinking?"

I could hear Bonnie talking in the background.

"It wasn't like that, Dad. You need to listen. I am in jail. I am very sick. I haven't slept in days. I haven't eaten. I am afraid. I keep passing out. This cell is all concrete. If I fall on it, I will split my head open. I am so scared. Please!"

"Sounds just like Christmas, Audrey. You are hooked on that stuff!"

"Forget Christmas; I need your help. I could die in here. Please!"

"Um, eh, wait a minute."

I heard Bonnie's shrill voice in the background saying, "You are not going anywhere, Mac. She is a junkie, and your blood pressure is up. You are not getting on a plane."

"Dad, you are a lawyer. I am your daughter. Why would you believe JB over me? Please, I am begging you!"

"I will see what I can do from here," he said, his voice strained. "Bonnie said my blood pressure is too high and it's too dangerous for me to fly."

Too dangerous to fly? In the last few years, my dad and Bonnie had taken several trips to Europe, including some Catholic pilgrimages to Medjugorje. They had just done a pub crawl across Ireland, for crying out loud!

This can't be happening. What am I going to do?

"Dad, if you don't come, I don't have a prayer of getting out! I'm going to die in here. How can you abandon me like this? You're my father!"

I heard Bonnie's voice in the background, telling him he was not stepping foot on a plane. I could hear the stress in his voice as he mumbled, "I'll see what I can do."

Then I heard a click. I stared in disbelief at the phone receiver.

I sat there, dumbfounded, not sure what to do next. The officer hurriedly pulled me to my feet and said, "Come on; let's go."

Tears ran down my cheeks as I allowed the officer to tow me down the hall. The officer abruptly stopped walking, and I felt a large hand shove me back into the cage. With my eyes cast down in humiliation, I walked over to the bench in the corner.

"What? No one coming to get you out?" one of the cellmates taunted.

I said nothing and continued to stare at the floor.

"Oh, don't want to talk about it? You will. It gets pretty boring in here," the same voice said with a snort.

"I just need my pain medication," I mumbled, "I have had a lot of surgery."

I heard several voices pipe up, saying things like, "Oh, yeah, baby." "We could all use some of the good stuff." "Right, you get some for us."

My face flushed with embarrassment as I willed myself to disappear. My temples were throbbing and my jaws were so tight I couldn't fully close my mouth. So I sat there with my jaws held slightly open, praying for relief. The pain seared through my neck and my entire back ached. I tried to hold myself steady, but my head was spinning and my vision was coming and going.

The look on my face must have revealed how sick I was. I shut my eyes.. The two girls across from me had been watching me. When I started to mumble and my upper body started to sway, they rushed over and sat on each side of me.

I heard one voice say, "This girl's really sick; get somebody!"

I felt two sets of hands gently turn me sideways and place my head on a lap. I could hear them pounding on the door, screaming, "She is not one of us! This girl is sick. Get a medic!"

I fell in and out of consciousness as I heard the shouts. When I woke up, they told me a medic did come in the cell, but he claimed I was faking. I couldn't discern their words as I slipped back into darkness.

They took turns cradling my head in their hands to secure it in their laps, saying soothing things. The girls I had looked on unfavorably at the beginning, the girls I had judged so quickly, were now my greatest gift. These girls I had feared a few hours ago had allowed compassion to overshadow their own problems and band together to help a stranger.

I had no idea how much time had passed, when my body went into convulsions. I was writhing on the floor when several officers rushed in and poked at me with sticks. When they realized that I was not faking, they lifted me into a wheel chair. My vision was blurry and my stomach was reeling as they whisked me to the infirmary of the maximum security wing. They dumped me on a thin mattress in a 10x10 concrete cell. I continued to fall in and out of consciousness, grateful for the silence.

THE SKY

SUDDENLY, THE CAR EXITED THE basement garage, and I was blinded by the light of day. I reflexively closed my eyes and then slowly squinted them open.

Dear God, look at the beautiful sky! It's breathtaking.

I craned my aching neck up to take it in. I was stunned at the stellar blue color against the soft, puffy white clouds.

I had lost track of time. I didn't know how long it had been since I had even seen through a window. I sat there enamored with the sight, taking it in, enjoying every second. The officers continued to drive through downtown—so many familiar buildings, people going about their everyday activities. It all looked so normal, so wonderfully normal.

They walked me up into the elevator and pushed the button marked psychiatric ward. I was so weak from sleep deprivation that an officer had to support me on each side for me to walk. They walked me into a small room with a plastic chair, placed me in the chair, removed my chains and left me. I heard the heavy steel door's lock turn from the other side. I was seated in a tiny room about six feet by eight feet with a locked door on either side. Wherever I was, it was just another cage.

There was a nurse with a clipboard behind a Plexiglas shield. She started to ask me questions and actually listened to my answers. It had been many days since I had been treated as a human being worth listening to. I was trying my best to answer the questions. I was making very little sense, but she seemed to know why I was there.

After I was checked in, she came around through the door and lifted me out of the chair. "Come with me," she said as we walked down a hallway. She turned into what resembled a hospital room and led me into the bathroom. "Let's get this dirty uniform off," she said as she helped me remove the prison jumpsuit. "I am sorry, but I can't leave you alone."

I just nodded as she glanced discreetly at my emaciated body and the bruises now turning yellow from the assault. Her eyes betrayed both compassion and outrage, but she made no comment. Instead, she wadded up the uniform and threw it in the trash. Then, she ran a bath and steadied me carefully as I climbed in.

"I think this is much safer for you, dear," she said. "You're too weak to stand in the shower."

It felt heavenly—the hot water racing over my lathered-up skin, running over my sore muscles. This nurse was an angel. She was so nice and handled me so gently. The nurse handed me a towel, a clean, soft, well-worn hospital gown, and footie socks. She led me carefully out of the bathroom and over to a bed. The room was six times as large as the cell I had just been in, and it had two real beds with blankets and pillows in it. And my God, it had a window. I walked mindlessly over to it. I could once again see the sky through the black bars. I took a minute to thank God while tears streamed down my face. He had rescued me from that awful concrete box.

I thanked the nurse profusely for her kindness. She kept staring at me with such pity in her eyes. She glanced quickly over my skinny body with such concern. She didn't know my story, but I saw the flash of anger in her eyes.

I lay down on the bed and prayed for two things: my animals' welfare and sleep. I was certain God wasn't going to let my animals die.

GOD SENDS MORE ANGELS

I KNEW I WAS IN A hospital and would finally get the medical attention I was in dire need of, but there were very disturbing sounds. Later, it was explained to me that since I was brought into the hospital straight from jail, I was still technically in custody. As a result, I had to be held in the maximum-security wing of the psychiatric hospital. This meant my fellow residents were people in two categories: they either suffered with a severe mental illness which caused them to pose a danger to themselves or others, and thus required immediate treatment and powerful medication, or they were particularly violent in nature and were considered dangerous.

The head psychiatrist allowed me to stay in my room for the first three days after he evaluated my level of trauma and fragile mental state. I was very content to lie in my room on the wonderful bed and stare out the window. It was bliss. I actually felt safe in this haven where no one was attacking me or accusing me of being an addict. No one was calling me a liar or turning their back on me. But then my respite was over. On the fourth day, I was told I had to attend all the group therapy sessions just like the rest of the patients.

My roommate at the time was on crutches. She had trouble getting around, but when she saw the fear in my eyes, she would go get my tray of food off the cart when it was meal time. Despite her injury, she managed to carry my food tray and lay it down on the bed and then she would leave so that I could eat in peace. I couldn't believe that someone could be so nice to me. At the time, it was the greatest of gestures.

I heard a gentle knock on the door. I jerked to a start. Who was this? It was not meal time. I looked toward the hall to see a small Hispanic man standing reticently in the doorway. Rafael was a patient. During subsequent therapy sessions, he would relay numerous incidents of physical abuse at a group home and his reluctance to return. I was taken aback by his story. Somehow, it didn't occur to me that a man would be afraid to go home.

Despite his meek disposition and cautious entrance, every bit of fear that I had managed to quell filled me again. My heart raced and my body stiffened as he entered my room. My eyes grew wide as I shrank back in fear when he came into view. As I lie there, my mind wondered if he started to hurt me, would the nurses get here in time?

Rafael had not seen me in the common room, and somehow, he knew why. Somehow, he sensed my fear. His eyes were full of compassion as he slowly entered my room. He stood as far away from me as he possibly could and looked in my eyes.

He then softly uttered these words: "You are broken, but you will heal."

There was an understanding in his eyes I had not seen from anyone else. Then, he gently placed a drawing on my bed and slowly retreated from my room. It took me several minutes to pull myself together. I finally reached out and pulled it over where I could see it. I just stared at it in disbelief.

It was a pencil drawing of a castle with large, open space surrounded by massive stone walls with turrets. Just outside the castle was a big anatomical heart with veins and arteries severed. As I stared at the mysterious drawing, the realization hit me. God was the castle on the left. I was the broken heart on the right. I was outside the wall, but there was an opening for me to go through. God was sending me a message. Healing was in reach.

THE REAL LAWYER

THE NURSE KNOCKED LIGHTLY ON the door. "There is someone to see you," he said as he walked away.

In the door stood a man I had never seen before. My eyes slowly took in his tall and stocky frame. Despite his business attire and gentle manner, I hastily backed away from him when he stepped into my room. When he saw the flash of fear in my eyes, he stopped and stood perfectly still.

After I collected myself, I asked, "Um, you are here to see me?"

"Are you Audrey Stewart?" he asked simply. Given his expression, I wasn't anything like what he expected.

I nodded my head slowly and watched him warily as he carefully took a few more steps towards me. Reflexively, I backed away again, a little slower this time.

"I am a lawyer, and I believe you are in need of one."

His strong frame was curtailed by his three-piece suit and calming voice. Although he was doing his best to keep his expression neutral, he was clearly as baffled as I was.

Since he had done everything possible to quell my fear, I tried to force myself to relax. "I'm sorry. I don't know who you are."

I suddenly remembered my manners and directed him to a chair in the corner. He sat down and set his briefcase on the tile floor. I was startled by the abrupt snap of the locks on the briefcase and his quick movements when he flipped it open. Perceiving my alarm, he drastically slowed his movements and cautiously removed his legal pad. He pretended to review his notes to allow me several minutes to collect myself.

"My name is Ross Moran. I am an attorney. Why don't you tell me what happened the day you were arrested?"

I rubbed my hands across the bedspread, trying to settle myself down. I cleared my throat and began to describe the events.

It was such a mess; where do I even start? Finally, I said, "I should start at the supposed Super Bowl party at my neighbor's house. Laney and Mitch had been my friends for like forever . . . ."

Mr. Moran interrupted, "I'm sorry. Excuse me for interrupting, but the arrest was on the twentieth of February, which was almost two weeks after the 'supposed party' as you refer to it."

"Yes, I know," I said. "But, the chain of events precipitated from the assault at a neighbor's house. And it is all linked to the divorce. I mean, my dogs were poisoned both times I was in divorce court."

Mr. Moran stopped writing and looked up from his pad. "Excuse me, your dogs were poisoned?"

"Yes, didn't they tell you?"

"Ma'am, I am a criminal attorney; the divorce is irrelevant to your case. The divorce is a civil matter."

"I know, but the day I was arrested was less than an hour after I called the detective on the assault case to have him add the dog poisoning incident to the file. Next thing I knew, a huge man was pounding on the door and came across the threshold and slammed me into the wall."

Mr. Moran looked down at a report and said, "OK, at least I have an explanation for why Animal Control was called." He flipped to the report and skimmed it quickly. "This report states that Animal Control picked up two large German Shepherds. But you are saying the officer rushed in your house and grabbed you and the dogs did nothing?"

He looked at me with incredulity.

"I know, it's a mess. My dogs were not able to defend me because they were so weak from the poison. I was in my own home. I mean; I am still not clear on exactly what I did wrong." I looked up at him, my expression searching for answers.

He immediately stopped taking notes, and looked up. "Do you mean to tell me that no one has informed you of the charges filed against you?"

"Um, something about trespass—that is why I started my explanation with that sham of a party. The detective said that Laney signed an affidavit stating that she gave me a formal criminal trespass warning several years prior, which is ludicrous. I mean, Mitch told me about the party that very morning; why would he mention it if I wasn't invited? And for Laney to claim that she gave me a formal criminal trespass warning years ago makes no sense. JB and I attended her private wedding in the Bahamas since then. And Dee and I worked together on her baby shower. I have no idea why she would say I was criminally trespassing; we hung out all the time."

Mr. Moran's expression divulged his considerable confusion. He tried once more: "OK, let's back up. Maybe I should begin with this: forget the trespass charge. It is the least of your problems. You are actually charged with a much more serious crime." He consulted his pad. "The charge is aggravated assault with a deadly weapon on a police officer. That particular charge carries a potential twenty-year prison sentence."

I just stared at him. My mouth dropped open.

"Ms. Stewart, someone had to tell you this. You really didn't know?"

"Well—um after I was attacked, I didn't sleep for days, then my dogs were poisoned . . . ," I trailed off as I pulled my knees to my chest. *What is happening? When I was arrested, all I cared about was my dogs.* I continued, "And then, shortly after I got back from court, my female was throwing up and my male dog could barely stand. So, all my energy was put toward getting the officer to wait for animal control to come get them. That is all I cared about. I assumed I would worry about charges later. All I cared about was saving my dogs."

Mr. Moran referred to the report in his lap. He looked up and said, "Well, this is making a little more sense. So, you are saying your dogs were gravely ill, so that was your only focus. I imagine the officer was quite confused himself." Finally, he saw some correlation between my story and the documentation in his file.

I thought a minute.

"Oh, you know. It is making more sense to me now. The officer was aggressive at first, but when he saw how sick my dogs were, his demeanor changed. Come to think of it, he was the one who pointed out that my female dog didn't even lift her head when he put me against the wall. And she was less than ten feet away."

"It says here that you filed charges for the assault and battery which took place at a neighbor's home. Apparently, the homeowners, a Mitch Suvell and his wife, responded by filing criminal trespass charges against you. They told the police they would drop the criminal trespass charge if you would drop the A&B charges. I don't have record that you dropped the complaint, so I assume that is why they issued a warrant for you."

I starred and said slowly, "What? Warrant? For me? There was a warrant for me?" I sat there and tried to replay the events in my head using the new information.

"So," I mumbled, "The officer who came pounding on the door and shouting at me thought he was picking up a . . . a criminal."

That is why the officer was so surprised my dogs were so sick.

Mr. Moran snapped me out of my thoughts by saying, "Some of this has to sound familiar. You are saying that you were never notified of the homeowners' filing criminal charges against you? Or informed that they offered to drop their charges if you dropped your complaint?"

I just shook my head no.

"You mean they didn't even notify you when the warrant was issued?"

I continued to shake my head in the negative. My mind was reeling; this was so much more serious than I thought.

Mr. Moran continued, "Well, I can't imagine the sheriff's office would not have notified you by phone at the very least before issuing a warrant. I don't mean to be indelicate, but you said you hadn't slept much. Is it possible you just forgot? "

"Not a chance. I was raised by a judge. Criminal charges, a warrant? This is the first time I am hearing any of this."

Mr. Moran just sat for a few minutes. "I'm sorry, but this is inconsistent with their policies. I can't imagine . . . ." He stopped talking and looked down and at his legal pad. "Oh, wait. Your husband, JB. He didn't file for divorce until after you were attacked?"

I nodded my head, still not able to form words.

After verifying the dates by flipping through the legal documents, he looked up and said, "So, all this happened within the last ten days or so. Did your husband happen to have remote access to the answering machine?"

I replied, "Sure." I hesitated a minute and said, "Hmmm . . . I haven't changed the access code since he left. I did wonder why I never heard back regarding the A&B charges, but once the attacks started on my animals, nothing else mattered to me."

The lawyer's expression changed and he seemed to have come to a decision. He stood and said, "OK, I think you need to hear this. You were not expecting me because you didn't call me. Your father did."

"My dad called you? You mean to help me?" I said happily. I sat up straighter; an enormous weight had been lifted off of my shoulders. Finally, this would all get straightened out.

"Well, not quite. Yes, your father wanted to retain me, but he insisted on one condition. I was to 'pretend to help you' and leave you in jail. Apparently this man, JB, has convinced your father that you are safer in jail." He sat back and gauged my reaction.

"What?" I couldn't believe what I was hearing. I slumped back down, completely deflated. I fought the tears; I didn't want to break down in front of a stranger.

Mr. Moran said, "In all my years as an attorney, no one has ever asked me to do such an outrageous thing. I don't breach my ethics for anyone. But it bugged me, and I guess I needed to see it for myself. Now that I am here, I can see you certainly need someone to help you. This is a confusing chain of events which happened in rapid succession, but I want to help you. Understand this: I flatly refuse to work for your family. But, if you can pay my fees, I will work for you."

"I'm sorry, what is the charge again?" I said, as I tried to grasp the enormity of the situation.

"Aggravated assault with a deadly weapon on a police officer. I can't imagine what happened to put you in this mess, but I can see you are a nice person. And you have clearly been through a terrible ordeal. I will need $7,500 for my retainer."

"That is a lot of money, but I can do it." I had to do it, I thought to myself. *What choice did I have?*

"Well, it is a serious felony. You will need more money for your bail bond, which is $65,000."

I had watched so many crime shows and was fascinated by the legal system. But, those words had never had such an impact. This was real, not TV. I could actually be back inside a jail cell for as long as twenty years. *Please God, no!*

VINCE AND JANET VISIT

MY HEART FILLED WITH HAPPINESS when I saw my two friends, Vince and Janet, enter through the locked door that separated me from the outside world. I worked with Janet at the start-up company and we had bonded commiserating over our severe back injuries. We would compare notes and we both appreciated talking to someone who had actually gone through it. Vince was her husband; his gentle nature was incongruous to his powerful build and shaved head. I hadn't really known them for that long, but they later confessed that they helped me simply because it was clear I had no one else and it was the Christian thing to do.

I rushed to greet them and threw my arms around Vince and then Janet. I was overjoyed to see them. It had been days since I saw a person that I knew, someone familiar who cared about me.

I tried to ignore the shock in their expression as their eyes scanned my battered and frail frame. Both Janet and I were doing our best to stop the tears.

I asked quickly, "My dogs, they survived?"

Vince said soothingly, "Yes, they are OK. All the animals are. The feeding instructions you placed at each entrance are comprehensive, so all of them are being taken care of properly. Just the way you would."

I just dropped my head and said a prayer of thanks. My dogs were OK; all the animals are OK; that was what mattered. The rest could all be straightened out.

Vince continued, "I found your handwritten Last Will and Testament on the printer. That really scared us. We had no idea things were that bad."

"I didn't mean to scare anyone," I said, "but after the attacks on me and my animals, I didn't want JB to benefit from an untimely death. That is why it was handwritten, to serve as a holographic will. I didn't have time to go to a lawyer to prepare it and get witness signatures. I am sure JB would contest it due to my mental state, but maybe it would give the police a place to start."

"Yes," Vince said, "I read it and saw that you bequeathed all your possessions to someone named Kathryn Johnson. Her number was included on your emergency contact list you placed with the feeding instructions, so I gave her a call."

"Wow, it worked," I said. "I made that list because I have friends from different activities, like work or competition. I always worried if something happened to me, they would not know how to contact each other."

I stopped abruptly. Vince pulled me from my thoughts, "What?"

"Well," I said, "JB has certainly taken most of my property, but I don't want anyone who is working with him gaining access to my property. I don't trust them around the animals."

"Well," Vince replied, "as you said, I only knew two people on that entire list."

I brightened and said, "I know! Maggie has a small side business that does embroidery. I will have her make up some hats that have some humorous message that no one would pay attention to. I will have the hats made and give you a list of people I consider trustworthy. That way, you won't have to say anything to anyone; if they are donning that ball cap, you'll know they can be trusted."

"Pretty good!" Vince replied with a laugh.

"So," I said, "that explains how Kathy knew where I was. She called this morning. I had lost touch with her over the last year when she and Arnie moved down south. She had no idea all this was happening. She is coming to see me tomorrow."

Janet asked, "How long since Kathy has seen you?"

I replied, "Oh, wow, at least a year. She retired and was very busy working with the builders for their house on the lake."

Janet must have thought that it would be a shock for Kathy. She said, "I would suggest that you warn her about your current condition, but no one could envision how weak and frail you look. Particularly anyone that knows you at all!"

KATHY AND ARNIE VISIT

WHEN KATHY ENTERED THROUGH THE door, I couldn't suppress my tears. She was my oldest and dearest friend. Kathy was my first boss when I relocated to Texas over twenty years prior and we had become very good friends. Her husband, Arnie, walked in behind her.

"They said you were in solitary confinement," Kathy said. "What was that all about?"

"Really?" I said, "I am not sure what happened. I was put in solitary confinement after I started having grand mal seizures. I think it was part of the infirmary."

She said, "Audrey, you don't have epilepsy."

I rubbed my temples and grappled to understand what had happened.

What would have caused those violent muscle contractions?

"Oh my God!" Kathy said. "It was withdrawal from all that medication. Good grief! I am so glad you are finally getting proper medical attention."

"I don't even know what day it is. How many days was I incarcerated? Wow, incarcerated. I never thought I would use that word in reference to myself."

"According to your next-door neighbor, you were arrested on the twentieth. It is now the twenty-fourth. You really don't know how long you were in jail?" Kathy said with mounting concern.

"I don't even know what day it is. In solitary confinement, there is no indication of night or day. There is no clock or time-keeping device at all. It seemed as if it was one very long excruciating day. It was awful." I shook in an attempt to rid myself of the memory.

"You don't remember how many nights you've slept?"

"The dim florescent lights in my cell were never turned off, so I wouldn't even know when it was time to sleep. Sleep eluded me the entire time anyway; the only rest I got was when I lost consciousness from the pain. Please, I don't want to talk about that. I am so grateful to be here, where there is a window, a real bed, and even a bathroom with a door."

Kathy said firmly, "Well, we need to make sure that you don't have to go back."

I looked at her, eyes wide with alarm.

Seeing the fear in my eyes, she said soothingly, "The doctors here are acutely aware that you are too weak to survive in that situation again. We will figure it out. I promise."

I hadn't considered that I would return to that sensory deprivation chamber, that stark, cold cage. I couldn't take it again.

THE DISABILITY CHECKS

THAT SAME DAY, MAGGIE CAME to visit. My eyes lit up when she walked through the steel door. I rushed over to her and hugged her. This was such a wonderful day; it had been so long since I had seen or talked to anyone that wasn't a cop or a health professional. But today I had visitors who actually cared about me. Tears ran down my face as I looked at Maggie. I led her to my room where we could talk.

"Oh, my God!" said Maggie. "I am so glad to see you! I was so worried."

I sat down with her and repeated the conversation with the lawyer. I turned to her and said, "Maggie, I need your help. I can't fix it from here. Please drive to my house and pick up my mail. I need my disability checks to pay his retainer. I will set you up on my account so you can deposit them. It would take two checks but they should be in my mailbox by now. They may be inside the house if my neighbor put the mail in the house."

We talked some more and then the nurse told me the thirty minutes was up and she had to leave.

A faded memory suddenly flashed in my mind: I am three years old, clinging to my mother and crying. She is in a psychiatric ward and the visiting time is up. I don't understand. Why are they taking her away? I screamed for them not to make me let go. The guards pulled me away from her and my dad takes my hand.

That was the last time I saw my mother.

"Are you all right?" Maggie asked.

"What, huh? Oh yeah, I will be."

I thought about how little I knew about my mother. I couldn't remember a family member ever mentioning her

153

name or referring to her in a story. All I really knew was she was supposedly either schizophrenic or bipolar, possibly both. I guess I had been conditioned not to ask questions. But now, it struck me how odd that was.

A few hours later, a patient came to my room and said I had a phone call. They handed me the community phone. Maggie said, "Audrey, there is no mail in your mailbox or in your house. I talked to Al and he thinks either JB is picking it up or having someone else pick it up. Can you think who?"

Wow, seriously? I thought for a minute and said, "Well, it probably wouldn't be Laney because she is involved in this mess up to her neck. The only person I can think of is Dee. I left a list of emergency contacts on my fax machine after I was assaulted. Both her work and her home number is on the list."

Two hours later, Maggie called back. "Well," she said, "I have good news and bad news. First, Dee did have the checks. I actually had to track her down at her place of business and demand them!"

"So, you got the checks. Great. What is the bad news?"

"I think you can cross Dee off your friends list!"

GROUP THERAPY

I T WAS TEN O'CLOCK, SO I was told to go out to the common room for the group therapy session. I sat down on the couch and grabbed a pillow and held it against me. Regardless of the situation, I always positioned myself as close to an exit as possible and held something in my hands that could serve as protection. I didn't even think about it anymore; it had become second nature.

One patient scared me more than anyone. I always kept my eyes averted and did everything I could to not engage him. Mark was about five-foot-eight with a well-muscled body covered in tattoos and dark hair cut close to his scalp. But, his most alarming trait was his stark cold eyes.

My fear was only slightly availed by the fact that the 'nurses' were all men, 'bouncer-types' even. Other than the dear little nurse who had helped me bathe when I first arrived, I didn't see another female nurse in that wing. It didn't take long to understand why this was necessary. The reason any one of them could double as a bouncer at any biker bar became abundantly clear when I witnessed them subdue a patient in the throes of a manic episode. Thank God for the facilitators!

THE ALTERCATION

THE LEADER OF OUR THERAPY sessions was Dottie, a female nun in her sixties who came in for that purpose alone. Dottie was a big gal, what my father would describe as "good Irish stock." My first couple sessions were fairly mundane, and by the third one I started to relax slightly.

Dottie started the session with, "Jennifer, why don't you start?"

Jennifer was a tiny little thing; she probably weighed less than one hundred pounds. She had beautiful skin, shoulder-length dark hair, and deep brown eyes. She was a natural beauty who needed little makeup. Unfortunately, her beautiful eyes usually held a vacant stare.

Jennifer was a gentle soul when her mind allowed her to rest. She was soft spoken and polite. She normally held her eyes down, almost apologetically. Jennifer was incredibly intelligent. Just the night before, we had been watching a game show in the common room and she answered every question correctly without even glancing at the television.

The patient who sat next to her was named Brian. He was a tall, lanky, reddish-haired young man with a boyish face. My guess was that neither Mark nor Brian were over twenty years old. All our eyes were on Jennifer as she started to speak, but, before she could get three words out, Mark was out of his chair and had straddled the coffee table to reach for Brian. I grabbed the pillow and was ready to shield my face if needed. To my astonishment, Sister Dottie jumped to her feet, simultaneously wrapping her sweater around her right arm and then extended it, hand opened, against Mark's chest. Apparently, Sister Dottie had sustained a bite or knife wound in a previous brawl and knew exactly how to protect herself.

Sister Dottie's substantial frame, coupled with the speed of her reaction slowed Mark down long enough to provide Brian an escape. Brian's lightning quick reflexes permitted him to vault backwards over the back of the couch before Mark could reach him. It was abundantly clear that both Brian and Sister Dottie had been in their share of confrontations. I sat there in horror, frozen, as the altercation played out only a few feet in front of me. My heart pounded and, despite my hands shaking violently, I kept a death grip on the pillow.

Sister Dottie stood fiercely between them while the "facilitators" raced to subdue Mark.

Dottie stood straight so that she was face-to-face with Mark. She was way too savvy to show any fear. "Mark, sit down. Control yourself. You are here to work on yourself, not on Brian!"

Mark was completely out of control now, most assuredly furious that his attack was thwarted by a nun well in her sixties. The nurses held him until the doctor could administer a shot and, after it took effect, they carried him back to the room they used for "detention."

And just like that it was over, but only because of Dottie's quick reaction.

What about next time? What if Mark comes after me?

To my surprise, Sister Dottie was about to resume the therapy session, as if nothing happened. Wow. What a trooper. But when she turned back to Jennifer, it was obvious that the altercation had awakened the demons in her head.

Sister Dottie said again, "Jennifer?"

Just then, Jennifer jumped to her feet and whirled around right and left, as if she was looking back to make sure no one was behind her.

"They're getting off the train!" Jennifer screamed. "No, stop! Get away from me!"

I knew how lonely it felt to be hallucinating and seeing something terrifying that no one else could see. To wage battle against an enemy while completely, utterly alone. I had to look away. I couldn't watch. I knew they were taking her to the "padded room." I had heard her tortured screams from there before. My heart ached for her as I silently said another prayer.

THE PRAYER CIRCLE

SINCE MARK WAS LOCKED UP in detention, I cautiously ventured out into the common room to eat dinner. I sat across from Brian and ate my sandwich. Brian and I looked up as we saw Jennifer headed to the food cart. She quietly pulled a tray and came over to sit with us. We both gave each other a concerned look. After a few minutes, we could assess by her demeanor that the demons had temporarily released her. Recognizing her discomfort, Brian turned the TV on to provide a distraction. We all faced the TV and chewed in silence. It was clear that Jennifer was willing herself to disappear into the worn cushions of the couch.

We each finished our sandwiches and carefully slid our trays into the bottom of the food cart. None of us had uttered a word. I looked at Brian, "I think I saw you write a prayer in your journal, right?"

"Yes, I did."

I gently moved closer to Jennifer and said, "It helps me to pray when I feel bad, Brian. Will you help us pray?"

I reached out my hand and Brian stood and clasped my hand. I held my hand down to Jennifer and looked at her. "Jennifer, will you help us pray?"

Jennifer looked up, a single tear track on her cheek. I will never forget the gratefulness in her eyes that someone saw her as a person. I knew exactly how she felt. I had been stripped of my humanity months ago. I nodded to her again and reached my hand out further. She slowly stood and held her hand out.

We all stood in a circle amidst the discord and confusion. I started to pray out loud. "Our Father, who art in heaven . . . ."

Their voices sheepishly joined mine and gradually became louder and our flimsy grips grew stronger with each word. One person came from the hallway and another, who had been sitting in the corner writing in a journal, quietly joined the circle. I kept my eyes closed as another hand gently separated my hand from Jennifer's so they could make another link. It was the most peace I had ever felt in that room. He was there with us, which made all of us feel better. If only that was enough to put an end to Jennifer's personal war.

My Turn to be the Angel

I HAD HEARD SOME NOISE IN the night but I didn't wake up. Incredibly, despite several full nights of sleep, I still had many weeks of lost sleep to make up for. Even after breakfast, I would return to my room and lay curled up in my bed most of the day. My rest was unexpectedly interrupted when Jennifer walked in and stood in the middle of the room. She just stood and stared at me.

My heart started to pound and my eyes grew wide. Several minutes passed, then suddenly Jennifer moved closer to me and pointed her finger near my face. I reflexively grabbed for my jaws to protect them.

"I saw you," Jennifer said accusingly. "I saw you today with your daughter."

A dread filled me as images of the facilitators dragging her to the "special room" flashed in my mind. I had heard her screams and the banging when she continually slammed her head against the wall. What was happening now? She was acting weird. Was she about to have a manic episode?

I didn't know what to do. I was afraid to yell for help because I was not sure how she would react. I certainly didn't want to startle her.

"I saw you with your daughter on the couch."

Oh no, this isn't good; she is hallucinating again. I pulled my covers up and shrank back, pressing myself against the wall.

I tried to keep my voice calm and said, "No, I am sorry. But you're mistaken."

We stared at each other for another several minutes, and then abruptly she turned and walked out of the room. I laid there, saying a prayer of thanks that nothing happened to me. I knew she wasn't malicious but I had witnessed her outbursts. My body couldn't withstand any more abuse. Whether she meant to hurt me or not was irrelevant.

I lay my head back down on the pillow, so grateful for the silence. I was by myself again. I was safe.

At dinner time, a girl I hadn't seen before walked in the room. As she entered, she glanced back at me over her shoulder and stopped in her tracks. Our eyes locked, the same look of confusion on our faces. I couldn't believe it.

What is going on? This is like looking in a mirror. She had the same color hair, the same length and cut. It was styled exactly like mine—shoulder length with bangs parted on the same side! She had the same delicate face features and bright blue eyes.

She even had the same body type. She was built curvy with a small waist and strong, muscled legs. She was a hair shy of five feet tall, just like me. We continued to stare at each other for several minutes, both of us speechless.

Then, something occurs to me. *Yes!*

"Do you have a daughter?"

My mirror image, Megan, stared back at me. She was confused but, at the mention of her daughter, she started to relax.

"Yes, she visited this morning. You must have seen her. Isn't she cute? She turned thirteen last week."

"Uh . . . yeah. Sure"

Megan's timid nature allowed me to feel safe around her. I didn't perceive any threat from her, so I began to talk with her. Perhaps because she seemed so familiar, it was like talking to myself, which was odd at first. But then, it felt very comfortable. Almost like I had a twin.

The similarities didn't end with our appearance. Megan confided in me that she too was enduring a horrible divorce. After our conversations, it was clear to me that her soon-to-be ex-husband was taking serious advantage of her mild nature and lack of knowledge of the community property laws. Megan was not as upset about losing the marriage as she was about figuring out how to provide for her daughter. She received disability pay, but it was not enough for her and her daughter to have a safe place to live. She wanted very little, just the old rental house on the edge of the property and the old truck she used for errands.

Megan was from a rural town and I was probably the only one in the downtown hospital who could have accurately calculated her husband's actual net worth. After days of talking with her, I decided to ask if she would let me help her calculate their community property.

"Megan, do you understand how the community property laws work?"

"Not really."

"First, did he own this property before you were married?"

"No, he bought it a couple years after."

"Awesome! Do you mind if I help you figure out what your assets are?"

"There is no use in that. I signed a prenuptial agreement not to go after his veterinary practice."

"Well," I said, "community property wouldn't be part of his vet practice."

Megan turned to look at me. "What do you mean?"

I pulled my journal over to my side and picked the pen up from the nightstand.

"You said there is property. How many acres and where is it located?"

"Well, about one hundred and fifty acres in Maytown"

"Is it heavily wooded or more like pasture?" I asked

"Oh no, it's mostly pasture, with beautiful old trees scattered about."

"What about fencing? Is it expensive pipe or wire and wood?"

"Actually, it is all pipe; it all matches. Like I said, it is really a pretty place."

"Hmm, does he cut hay on it?" I asked.

Megan said, "Well, actually he has someone bale it a couple times a year."

"Bingo, land generates revenue from hay," I muttered. "Do you own any cattle?"

"Yes, we do."

"OK, how many? Can you describe them for me?"

"Oh, at least one hundred," Megan said, "but I don't know how to describe them."

I thought for a few minutes trying to figure out how to determine what they are worth. I explained, "Cattle are like dogs; there are different breeds. Also, some cattle are worth a lot more than others"

"Why?"

"Well," I thought about the best way to explain. "OK, cattle are sold by the pound. And, certain breeds are really good beef cattle, so they are twice as heavy as the others. So, the most expensive cattle are the breeds that are real stocky. Um, like the difference between a greyhound and a pit bull."

"Oh, I get it. They are definitely stout, and they are all black."

I stopped writing for a minute and looked up. I said "All black? So, pretty shiny coats and short and compact."

"Yes, exactly!"

I started to calculate on my pad. I said, "Jackpot! A herd of Angus cattle. You said you have about one hundred total?" I finished my calculation and started a new section on the pad. "If he has that many cattle, he must have a way to transport them, right?"

Megan thought and said, "Oh, like that really long trailer Doug keeps behind the barn. He doesn't use it hardly at all."

"Perfect! Is it aluminum?"

"Um, I am not sure what you mean?"

"There are two types of trailers: steel and aluminum. The aluminum trailers are several times as expensive and retain their resale value."

"I have no idea at all what it is made of," Megan said.

I stroked my chin with my hand and said, "I am almost certain it would be aluminum, hmmm. Oh, I know! Does it look painted like a car or shiny, sort of reflective? Like that aluminum foil you use for cooking."

"Yes, shiny. I think he bought it about two years ago."

"Triple decker!" I mumbled as I add another significant amount to the list. "OK, this is great. This will be pretty accurate. I am assuming he has big truck to pull it. Is it a diesel?"

"I am not sure."

"Come on," I said encouragingly, "don't quit me now. You are doing great. We are almost done! Is the truck loud or quiet like a car?"

"That one is easy," Megan said with a laugh. "It is very loud."

"Is it a crew cab?"

Megan looked at me with confusion.

"Sorry, is it a two-door or four-door?"

"Oh, four-door," Megan answered, "and it is only a few months old."

"Just one more thing. Is it four-wheel drive?"

Megan looked confused and said, "Gosh, how on earth would I know that?"

"Is there a big gap between the top of the tire and the bed of the truck?" I asked as I spread my fingers apart. "You know, like this much."

"Yes, exactly!"

"Crew cab, diesel, 4x4." I mumbled to myself as I added it to the tally. "Sixty thousand, easy."

I summed up all the numbers I had scribbled on the page, and the total of the marital assets was over 350,000 dollars. I showed Megan the page with the total and watched her face with amusement. She looked at me with astonishment. I explained the prenuptial agreement did not protect assets that her husband purchased after they were married. The marital assets such as the ranch, cattle, and equipment were now community property. That meant she was entitled to half.

"But I don't even have a lawyer," Megan said uncomfortably. "I don't think I have the strength to fight this battle. If I did, I wouldn't be in here."

If anyone in the world understood this, it was me.

"It's OK. You probably don't need one. When his lawyer realizes that you now understand what your rightful share is, he will probably just want to get you to agree to a small sum quick."

I told her to get on the phone to her sister who would get a message to the husband's lawyer informing him that she was now rooming with a family law attorney who explained to her the community property laws. Tell him that, as luck would have it, the attorney grew up on a ranch and knows exactly what these types of marital assets are worth. I wrote a few sentences down on a paper to give her a cheat sheet. I told her to use phrases like "marital assets" and "community property."

For the first time since I had known Megan, she seemed hopeful. But then Megan seemed to lose her courage at the last minute. She looked at me. "I don't know."

"Think about it," I said. "He has his vet practice, which is what he is so afraid of losing. You only want the rental house and your truck. If you say you are willing to settle for only that so you and your daughter have a place to live, Doug knows he comes out on top. If he doesn't, I am sure his attorney will explain it to him."

I continued, "Make sure you really sell it. Tell them with all the fight you can muster he is getting off easy. You could easily go to court and he would lose another $200,000, potentially even more with a sympathetic judge. They are going to see a single mother on disability against a rich veterinarian with a half million in personal assets over and above his vet practice."

Megan was about to dial the phone, and I stopped her.

"Wait. Doug sounds like a bully, so he has to think he is getting something over on you. Tell his attorney you demand 100K in addition to the house and the truck. Then, when you agree to take only the house and truck, it will sound like a better deal."

I wrote a script for her and she made the call. She was pretty nervous, but every time she glanced at me, I just shook my fist. I kept nodding to her. When she was done and the attorney started to argue with her, I told her to hang up. She did. Megan looked at me in disbelief.

Megan jumped up clasping her hands. "It might just work," she said. "The lawyer was really taken aback. He seemed astounded that I would use phrases like marital assets and community property."

For the first time, Megan had a broad grin and a sparkle in her eyes.

"Thank you," said Megan. "I have to tell you, that felt so good!"

Prior to meeting Megan, I felt so beaten down and my spirit was broken, truly broken. Rafael had called it correctly. I used to be absolutely fearless. I would get on any horse, no matter what the behavior: bucking, rearing, etc. I never hesitated before I climbed up in the saddle and applied the necessary correction to "fix" the horse so it was safe for its rider. I would go into an extremely dangerous equine event and do it with speed and style. I never drove into work doubting I would be resourceful enough to tackle the job.

As always, He provided. Helping Megan, in essence, was helping myself. God literally held up a mirror which revealed I was but a shadow of my former self. Due to my experience competing in cattle events, I was in the unique position to ascertain the value of her marital property. It was up to me, and only me, to help her get her rightful share.

I pushed my problems aside and dug down deep to find the strength and resourcefulness I had thought was gone forever. It reminded me of the fire I used to have inside, the passion for life. Yes, it was still there. No one could take that away. Not EVEN JB!

MY BODYGUARD

I BEGGED FOR PERMISSION TO NOT join the therapy sessions after Mark's attack on Brian. The staff understood how fearful I was, but they were bound by the rules for a patient that was "in custody." I sat next to Sister Dottie and fretfully prayed I would not get pulled into a physical altercation. I stayed away from Mark at all times and didn't dare make eye contact. I always held a pillow ready to shield my face from a thrown object or fist. If I didn't have to be in the common room, I relished being alone and safe in my room.

One morning when I walked back to my room after session, my worst fear was realized. I turned the corner and Mark was standing in front of my door. My heart started pounding.

Oh, my God! What do I do now?

I thought about Sister Dottie. And, before I knew it, I stepped right up to him and got in his face.

"You know what I am in here for?" I said.

Mark said with a smirk, "Something silly."

I moved even closer to him. I was inches away from his face; I could feel his hot breath on my forehead. I looked straight into his eyes and said, "Aggravated assault with a deadly weapon on a police officer! What about you? Somebody steal your pink skateboard? Huh?"

His mouth fell open and he stepped back. "Nah, you didn't."

I jerked my head to the side like I have seen on TV and stepped right back up into his face. I whispered in a raspy voice, "Yeah, that was me."

Suddenly, the hard look in his eyes disappeared and gradually changed to one I can only describe as respect.

Mark had cornered me and something snapped inside me. I decided to get his attention in the only way he understood. All at once, my fear was gone. I was finished being pushed around; I was finished being afraid.

If I was going to die, then I was going down with a fight.

I had followed all the rules, and look where I was: in the maximum-security wing of the psychiatric hospital, facing twenty years. I had counted on people and they clearly let me down. It was up to me, only me. Certainly, no one else was going to do it. I didn't live through multiple surgeries, a suicide attempt, the betrayal of my husband and family, and the dangerous withdrawal from numerous psychiatric drugs to die now—particularly to have my life ended at the hand of some random gangbanger. There was some reason I was still alive and I needed to figure out exactly what that was.

After that altercation, Mark appointed himself my protector. He eventually told me his story and I told him mine. He was astounded that, until a few months ago, I had never been near a jail or had a warrant issued for anything. When he knew the whole tragic story, he had even more respect for the fact that I was able to summon the courage to call him out that day in the hallway.

One day, I noticed a recent arrival walking down the corridor in my direction. Dana was very thin, with a plain face and mud brown hair. She walked up to me with Mark a few steps behind her. He shoved her forward and said, "Go ahead, tell her."

"Well," Dana said reluctantly, "um—you know when you had that conversation with your lawyer. Well, I . . . ."

"Now!" Mark interrupted.

"Well, I put it on speaker phone. That is why everyone knows your business."

"And . . . ," Mark said sternly.

"Well," Dana said, "I'm sorry. Mark explained about your husband and all that stuff and I am totally sorry. I shouldn'ta done it. It was mean." Then, she looked at Mark for permission and quickly walked away.

"Mark," I said, "I appreciate you sticking up for me. But you didn't have to do that."

"Yeah I did. What she did wasn't right and she needed to apologize."

And, there it was. The person everyone in the wing feared had become my protector. Once again, He sent someone to teach me something. This troubled kid, this dangerous kid, I finally saw as a person. Mark confided the details to his story and it was horrible. No one ever believed in him or showed him how to become a good man. He was just another misunderstood, lost soul. It was clear he wanted to be liked but fear was all he knew. He put down his shield and exposed his vulnerability to me. Out of everyone I'd met, he's the one I worry about most.

EILEEN STEWART

THE CONFESSION

I KNEW IT WAS MY LAST group therapy session before I left the hospital, so I had one thing left to do.

When it was my time to share, I said, "I know I haven't said that much in here. To be honest, I didn't believe I belonged here. I couldn't imagine what I would have in common with any one of you. But, one by one you shared your stories and bared your soul." I sipped some water and braced myself, fighting the tears. "But this has been an incredible journey for me.

"When I was in solitary confinement, all by myself with no one to react to, I came to a very disconcerting realization. When I got right down to it, I didn't really like myself as a person. I have lived life at warp speed and filled my every moment with constant distractions. If I wasn't at work, or training for the next competition, I was at happy hour downing a few drinks to calm my inner self.

"I realized I had carefully honed three personas—the professional, the competitor, and the entertainer—and they were all masks. None of them were the real me. And when I was left with the real me, I realized I simply played the role necessary to be the person that people would love.

"But when I was in solitary confinement, I was a lead actor without an audience. All the boundaries and expectations for being an employee, an athlete, a wife, a daughter—they were all gone.

"So, I was rudderless. Then I listened to your stories and I realized that I had it all backwards. Instead of living to please everyone else, I needed to become the person I wanted to be, and then surround myself with people who like me for who I am, not my performance.

"You have taught me to value others, and when I ask a stranger, 'How are you?' to actually stop and listen to the answer. Maybe, just maybe, I could even try to help. Maybe I could speak from the heart instead of just my mouth."

I cleared my throat and continued. "Like all of you, I've hit rock bottom in here. I have no one left to impress. Now, all I want is to become the best version of me and fulfill the purpose God gave me. I need to start over and rebuild myself from the inside out. So, I thank you from the bottom of my heart, not only for listening, but for generously sharing your lives and baring your soul to a complete stranger."

They all clapped and stood. Tears flowed freely as one broken soul after another hugged me. We found healing in the accepting and by embracing the brokenness of another, which allowed us to accept it in ourselves. I knew it was the first day of a new kind of life. A better life.

As I was leaving, I turned to look for Mark. I could see he was talking to his parents. Standing with his parents, it was evident just how young he was. He caught sight of me and whispered to them. I saw them nod their head and he trotted over to me. He looked down and shuffled his feet.

"I'll miss ya," he said quietly.

"Are you going home?" I asked.

He looked back at his parents. With embarrassment he said, "No, they don't think I am ready."

I looked at him with fondness; that same man I had been terrified of now looked like a little boy.

"They are wrong; you are a good kid. Don't ever let anyone tell you that you are not worth it. OK?"

Mark looked away, unsure of how to handle my kindness. I grabbed his face and turned it back to me. "I mean it! You are a good man, with a good heart. Don't let anyone make you forget that!"

He raised his head up and said, "Yeah, OK."

As the suffering prophet Job once said: "For the thing which I greatly feared is come upon me."[1] Deep down in my subconscious, I had always been afraid of becoming like my mother and ending up in a psychiatric hospital. And yet, it was in the place of greatest dread that I found my redemption.

---

1 The Holy Bible, King James Version. Cambridge Edition: 1769; King James Bible Online, 2017. www.kingjamesbibleonline.org.

THE NECKLACE

AFTER ALMOST TWO WEEKS IN the hospital, the officers came into the ward to take me back to jail. They had the shackles with them, but when they started to put them on me, I heard someone clear their throat loudly. We all looked behind us to see the head psychiatrist with a stern look shake his head. They obeyed and walked me out of the hospital without any chains.

After a thirty-minute drive, the car cruised from the bright daylight down into the dank dark garage under the jail. I tried to push down the fear, but I felt my stomach lurch as the car stopped. With an officer's arm under my shoulder, I stepped out of the car. The driver came to my other side and I was guided towards a plain steel door.

The officer knocked twice, and the door was opened from the other side. With an officer on each side, I was escorted through the short hallway into a small elevator. When the door opened, I was led through narrow hall after narrow hall. At the end of each hallway was a heavy steel door. And after I passed through each one, I heard the noise I had become so accustomed to: the sound of the deadbolt sliding into the locked position.

The officers, who looked slightly familiar, each stared at me in disbelief. The hospital doctors had been able to control the pain and the excruciating headaches, allowing me to enjoy several days of uninterrupted sleep. I had relished the glorious, wonderful sleep. Something I was now so grateful for, but had always taken for granted. I no longer suffered from delusions; I no longer heard voices.

Prior to this situation, I had never been in any trouble. Therefore, the police had never met me before. The only person they knew was the unstable person in the throes of a psychotic break, resultant from PTSD and the effects of powerful anti-psychotics. Each officer I passed had the same look of astonishment. My golden hair was clean and shiny and a natural glow replaced the gray pallor of my skin. The empty stare had been replaced with sparkle in clear blue eyes.

Perhaps the most striking difference: I was walking under my own power. The day the officers checked me into the hospital, I was so weak I couldn't stand unassisted. To get to the squad car, I required an officer to support me on each side. But now, I had a long stride and purposeful walk and held my head high.

Each expression contained recognition of how far I had come. So, with each step, each look of amazement, I grew more confident and regained another piece of my former self. I was still very thin and very weak, but my resolve had returned. And every one of them could see it.

Once I was in the booking area, I was told to sit on a bench. An officer came to get me and told me to follow him to be "processed" out. We stepped through a door and into an office. My eyes lit up when I saw Kathy waiting for me. I was so happy to see her. Kathy had worked with my lawyer to arrange my bail and provide the necessary paperwork to expedite my release.

The officer handed me a yellow envelope with my name on it. I opened it and grabbed my purse from inside. I searched it, and then dumped the contents out on the desk. I ran my hand around the envelope to make sure it was empty.

"Wait," I said with alarm, "I had a gold necklace. It had the image of Jesus, the Divine Mercy one. My father gave it to me years ago. I never took it off! Not since the day he gave it to me."

The officer looked up and said, "You say it was gold? Solid gold?"

The implication was clear. If it wasn't in the envelope with my other belongings, it was gone. My heart sank to think I would never see that necklace again. It had saved my life on the terrible day when I took all those pills. Without the metal emblem with the curved edges biting into my breast bone, I don't think they would have been able to bring me back.

"It's OK," Kathy said, "Audrey, let's go home."

I dropped my head, and followed her towards the exit, but just as I reached the door, another officer hurried into the office and said, "Ma'am."

I turned around to see a young man in uniform with dark hair. He looked at me and then down at his right hand. I followed his glance and was stunned when I saw what was in it. The lights were glinting off the shiny gold medallion of Jesus, the chains spilling over from his palm.

"I think this is yours."

My eyes filled with tears. "Thank you so much. You have no idea what this means to me."

I dropped my things on the floor and hurriedly placed it around my neck and hooked the clasp.

"How in the world did he know that was yours?" Kathy asked.

"I know how," I said as I touched it to my chest and said a quiet prayer of thanks. It was the sign I needed to know everything would be all right.

EILEEN STEWART

HOME

KATHY PULLED HER CAR INTO the driveway of my beloved ranch. I reveled in the familiar sound of the gravel crunching under the tires. My eyes searched the property to find my dogs. I had been told that they had lived through the ordeal, but I wasn't sure what to expect.

Kathy read my mind and said, "Al wanted to greet you, so he is in the house with the dogs."

Al was a retired postmaster and my neighbor of more than twenty years. I could picture him sitting out on the deck during one of our countless lazy conversations. Al was a kind, intelligent man, with deep brown eyes that would light up when he told the latest tale of a cherished pet. He had been someone I could count on from the day I moved into that neighborhood. He loved his big red Massy Ferguson tractor and used it often to help someone in the neighborhood. Either he was using it to turn the dirt over in my arena or to remove a tree that had fallen from a storm. Al was always there to lend a hand, particularly when I had a task I wasn't able to do for myself. I felt as if he thought of me as a daughter. His house sat on top of the hill, just inside the entrance of the neighborhood. Everyone felt safer knowing Al was on sentry duty.

I heard the front door open and the sound of my dogs' paws pounding the wooden deck. Their yelps of delight filled the air. In one leap, they barreled down the stairs and made giant strides to reach me. My heart was restored when I saw their shiny coats and bright eyes. They looked so regal and strong. They had fully recovered! I dropped to my knees, overcome with gratitude. When they reached me, I wrapped my arms around their wriggling bodies, buried my face in their fur, and rolled around the ground with them. Tears of joy streamed down my face.

When the dogs finally let me up, I headed straight to the barn. They trotted happily at my side. Amazing. Just a few weeks prior, I was sure I would never get to do this again. The simple task of walking to the barn to feed my horses meant so much. I slid the main door open and took in the beautiful sight. My two gelding's heads jutted out over the stall gates. Their eyes were bright as they stomped their feet and nickered to me. I slid the nearest stall door open and threw my arms around my old gelding, Mister T. He reached out and grabbed my jacket and held it tightly between his teeth.

"What is he doing?" I heard Kathy say from behind me, her voice somewhat alarmed.

I swallowed hard and tried to speak. After a few minutes I said, "He is telling me he is not letting me go. He doesn't want me to leave him again."

It would take a train to drag me away from him again. This horse and I had been through what seemed like a war together. His faith in me was unwavering. I laid my face on his back, with one hand stroking his chest and the other on his hip. I was filled with contentment as my head rose and fell softly with his breath.

A feeling of tranquility washed over me as the events of the last few months melted away. I was home where I belonged. I finally gently removed my hands from Mister T and headed to the bright yellow barrel which held their feed. They started nickering excitedly as I poured the grain in their feed troughs. I walked into Magic's stall and stroked his warm, soft nose while he happily chewed his grain. I had returned to the world I understood and loved. I turned to Kathy with a broad grin.

"Let's get you inside," Kathy said. "You probably should rest."

I looked at her and she returned a familiar stare. The one that meant arguing was futile. I laughed to myself and shook my head. I had seen that look many times over the last twenty years, so I obediently followed her out of the barn. As I walked up the steps and approached the front door, I was surprised to see a bright pink official notice nailed to the front door. I had no idea what it was. I read it and turned to Kathy with panic in my eyes. I then looked over at Al, but he had purposely looked away.

"Yes," Kathy said calmly, "we know about this. The house is in foreclosure."

My voice cracked. "This says it has been already scheduled for auction. This is not possible; the mortgage payments were supposed to be auto-debited out of the joint account! JB moved out less than two months ago. No, there must be some mistake. "

"No," Kathy said gently, "it is right. I called the bank. Apparently, the house payment hasn't been made for over six months."

"Why didn't you tell me?"

"Audrey, you almost died. You needed rest. I knew you would not be able to rest if you knew this. You are free now and we can see what we can do." She was right, of course, but it did nothing to alleviate my anxiety.

She grabbed my arms again and said, "There is more. The house is pretty empty. JB took everything he wanted when you were in jail. We will have to clean it up as soon as the utilities are back on. Those bills weren't paid either." I had dropped my head and my eyes were looking down. Kathy put her hand under my chin to look straight in my eyes. "Audrey, it is done. There is no use getting upset. It is just stuff that can be replaced and at least, for now, you still have a house to live in. I need you to focus on your immediate problems. You are out on $65,000 bail and are facing twenty years in prison!"

"Sorry Audrey," Al said, "I guess he got whatever was left. JB asked me if he could store some stuff at my house several weeks ago, but I refused."

I looked at Al confused and asked, "When was that?"

Al answered somberly, "After they took you in the ambulance."

"You mean when I was in the hospital fighting for my life!" I said with incredulity.

Al just shook his head and looked down at his feet.

As I processed what he said, I stopped and looked back at him. "Hold on; you mean he was moving stuff out of the house even before he filed for divorce?"

I thought back to when I walked in the door after being dropped off from the hospital.

"Oh, now it makes sense."

"What?" Al asked.

"When I walked in from being dropped off from the hospital, JB's face was red and it looked like he had been sweating. That must be when he moved all the expensive photography equipment I bought! No wonder all the color drained from his face when I walked in. I probably missed him in action by minutes!"

Al and Kathy locked eyes and then looked away. They were embarrassed for me. They could see how crestfallen I was. I thought JB loved me, and look at how it ended. What a fool I was.

"OK," I said to Al with frustration, "but after you knew that, why did you let JB on the property the day I was arrested?"

"Because JB showed up with a truck," Al said a little defensively. "He said he checked the law and, since he was still residing there, he had a right to go into the property. Then, he told me if I didn't get out of his way he was going to drive the moving truck through the fence." Al continued, "Audrey, I really had no idea what to do. I didn't want him to damage your property. I know how much you love this place and I have watched year after year the work you put in it. JB even threatened to go get the police if I didn't stand aside. I guess I figured whatever it took to get him out of your life would be worth it."

"I guess I don't have to check the garage," I said. "I am sure it is empty—well except for my new lawn tractor. He wouldn't have any use for a 26hp mower in an apartment."

"Actually, that is gone too," Al said reluctantly.

I looked at him with astonishment. "What? You mean he took my new lawn tractor?"

Al pointed down the road. "Actually, it didn't go on the moving truck. I watched Mitch drive it right down the road towards his and Laney's house."

I dropped my head and kept walking.

Kathy said to me, "Yes, everything is gone, but you are still here. Audrey, you are alive!"

"Yes, that's what matters!" Al said perking up, "We can't believe you lived through this! I helped Kathy clean out your bathroom; we had several large trash bags of prescriptions. My God!"

"Yes, I had no idea what you were taking," Kathy said. "It was incredible. I can't believe you were taking all that medication at once! I looked some of it up: mood enhancers, anti-psychotics, real powerful stuff. And then, you went cold turkey after you were arrested, which is probably what caused the grand mal seizures in jail."

"Yeah, they actually landed me in solitary confinement."

In an effort to shake the bad memory, I said, "Well, you don't have to worry about getting rid of the Xanax, I did dispose of them the hard way. My agitated state when I visited Maryland was largely due to them. I apparently had a reverse reaction to it."

"Sheesh," Al said, "that is all you needed. I am sure the Xanax's interaction with the other ten or fifteen medications in your system didn't help." He just shook his head. "I will never forget that terrible night!" he said, referring to the night of my suicide attempt. "I was watching the news and saw the flashing lights go by, so I went out on my porch to see where they went."

Kathy looked at Al and said, "I didn't know you were here."

"Yes," Al said, "I went out on the porch and watched the flashing lights and saw they turned in here. So, I threw on a jacket and came right away."

I looked at Al and said, "That can't be right; JB gets home at 5:15 without fail. I remember distinctly it was 3:00 when I took the pills, I wanted it to be over by the time JB got home."

"No," Al said with certainty, "it was dark out; it must have been 7:30 or 8:00. I remember being surprised that he didn't get in the ambulance with you."

"He must have followed it in his car," I said.

Al corrected me. "Actually, he sat on the couch with Mitch and Laney. Laney was patting his leg and saying something about how much better off he would be if you died."

Kathy and I turned and looked at him. We said in unison, "What?"

Al went on to say, "I couldn't believe it either. Your next-door neighbor was here, too. When we heard what Laney said, she and I locked eyes. She walked right by me on the way to the door mumbling, 'I can't listen to any more of this.'"

I just dropped my head. *How embarrassing.* I was supposed to be smart. How did I let this happen?

"I'm sorry," Al said, "I shouldn't have mentioned it. I thought you knew."

Words failed me, so I just squeezed his arm and slowly walked away.

MAKING MY WAY BACK

KATHY STAYED WITH ME FOR several weeks. I was still very weak and fearful, but grateful to finally be home in my own bed. Sleep was still difficult; my brain continued to replay that terrible beating. I still had an overwhelming fear that my attacker would return, but not being alone helped immensely. But I knew she couldn't stay forever. I was going to have to figure out how to live on my own.

I used to be a big fan of the crime shows, the who-dunnits, if you will. My heart would always go out to the victim of a violent attack. These shows would often portray this character in a perpetual state of shock and disbelief, who lived in constant fear that their assailant would return. A few of the victims would even become shut-ins and never regain the courage it took to leave their home. As much compassion as I felt for them, I never understood how debilitating that type of trauma could be following an assault. My heart went out to them, but I couldn't help but think that if they worked hard enough with someone knowledgeable, they would be able to overcome it.

I finally understood. I mean really understood. So, I dealt with it the only way I knew how. If I was working with a traumatized horse, I would gradually desensitize it to whatever had caused the trauma. For example, if a horse panicked every time they heard a plastic bag crackle in the wind, I would gradually expose him to it until it was so familiar that I could actually groom them with it.

I would begin with putting the horse in his stall where he felt safest and place a white plastic bag directly under his feed trough. I would use a brightly colored bag to make sure it was visible against the bedding. I would also weigh it down and secure it so that it wouldn't move or make noise. I would drop the feed in the bucket and position myself where I could stroke the horse when he summoned the courage to venture up to get a bite of grain.

I would let the horse determine the pace and get a bite of feed when he was ready. When he was able to calmly go up to the feed bin and ignored the bag, I would move it from the very corner and closer to the horse. Eventually, it would be positioned where it would require the horse to step on the bag to get to his grain. The first time he stepped on it and it crackled, he would probably shy away and snort. However, since his flight was uninhibited, he would calm down quickly. Over time, he would figure out nothing happened to him when the bag crackled, and the level of his reaction would decrease over time. Once he figured out that the noise was caused by him stepping on the bag, and he was in control, he would relax even more.

Ultimately, the horse would ignore the bag entirely. At this point, I would gently slip the bag over my hand and use it to rub his back and shoulders while he ate his grain. The bag would still make a crackling noise, but now the horse associated the noise from the plastic to positive things, eating grain and being massaged. Even though this method took a couple of weeks, it was the best way I devised over many years to help a horse through trauma.

I decided to apply the same methodology to my healing. I had to desensitize myself to being outside of my comfort zone: my house. So, I started the painstaking process of convincing myself that no harm would befall me once I stepped outside the walls of my safe haven. With stopwatch in hand, I left the back door wide open and stepped out on the deck for thirty seconds. Despite my heart pounding and sweat breaking out on my forehead, I forced myself to wait until the thirty seconds had passed.

Then I raced back inside and slammed the door as I slowly sank to the floor. I sat there with my arms tight against my chest, and waited for my heart rate to return to normal. I then did something around the house to keep my mind off of it. After an hour or so, whatever I needed to calm down completely, I repeated the exercise. I continued this process as often as I could each day. As I could tolerate it, I increased the duration of standing on the deck by thirty seconds, then one minute, and then two minutes. This sounds trivial but it was incredibly difficult. It took all my energy to force myself to wait until the allotted time had passed.

I worked with myself as if I were that horse. If I regressed and became too panicked, I backed off the time and went back to a duration I knew I could handle. After I could stand on the porch for five minutes without breaking into a sweat, I closed the door until it had only a few inches of gap. If I could still see a sliver of my couch, I knew I could shoot through the opening if someone approached. Eventually, I closed the door all the way. Next, I stood a few feet from the door. Gradually, I moved farther and farther away from the door until I could reach the barn all by myself. That was a very good day indeed!

After I was able to walk to the barn, I resumed my daily feeding routine I loved so much. My neighbors had fed them for many weeks, but little by little, I took over the duties. I always had a cell phone in my pocket and my little .38 tucked behind me in the waist of my jeans. But each time my horses ran up to me, chasing each other and kicking up their feet, my heart healed a little more.

It was almost a month before I could walk out to the barn when it was dark, but I did it. When I finished feeding, I raced into the house and slammed the door. My body trembled and my heart raced. But with each trip, I recovered a little faster. Now that I could take care of my own animals, I had to find a way to save the ranch. The foreclosure was on hold, but I needed to make a pile of money fast or it was gone. I said a prayer that something would come along.

ANGER MANAGEMENT

IN ADDITION TO THE OUTPATIENT group therapy, I was ordered to complete an anger management class. I had heard about anger management classes before; however, I really thought that I would reach the end of my life without a court mandating my attendance at one.

I had no idea what to expect as I slowly drifted into the parking space in front of the plain-looking building with Suite B written across it in big blue letters. As I got out of my sporty, late-model car, I immediately felt out of place. I could feel eyes following me as I made my way between a Harley motorcycle and a pickup truck with low-profile tires hidden beneath a layer of dust.

As I walked in the entrance, I paused a minute to take in my surroundings. Several people were seated in old steel chairs loosely arranged in a semicircle. They all wore similar expressions, some variation of "let's get this over with." The group consisted of mostly heavily muscled, tattooed men with shaved heads and torn jeans (which I expected). However, there were also a few teenagers and two females who were diminutive in size and timid in nature.

It wasn't until I sat down that I noticed a line of people up at the front. The girl across from me saw my confusion and said, "Oh, you need to go pay."

The class "tuition" was sixty dollars, which could be paid by cash, money order, or in six monthly installments. I grabbed for my checkbook and the instructor looked at me with skepticism and said, "Oh no, we only take cash."

I wasn't ready for that. Apparently, I was no longer a part of society that was trusted to have money in an account to cover a personal check. Luckily I had a ten dollar bill to cover the first installment.

As I walked over to take a seat, a very tall, well-built man entered through the door. When I crossed in front of him, he stopped and looked down at me.

He asked, "Who are you: the teacher?"

"No, I am one of you."

His expression divulged he didn't believe me. I should note that by the end of the class he was a believer.

Since it was the first night, the instructor wanted each person to talk about the situation which necessitated this class and the actual charges they were facing. This was all very new to me. I was now painfully aware that my charge was pretty serious and the last thing I wanted to do was to have to say it out loud in front of a group of strangers.

So, with my little size-six foot nervously tapping, I watched the clock tick away, waiting for eight o'clock to arrive. As each person told their story and said their charge, several minutes ticked by. As they spoke, I realized most of these people were like me and that they had simply made a mistake. Then, as each one went, it became more obvious that no one's charge was anywhere near as serious as mine. Now I was intently watching the clock, praying silently that somehow, I would escape the pending embarrassment.

Luckily, the instructor didn't go in any order. She would randomly ask people to go when someone else finished. *How perfect is this? There is no way she can accurately keep track of who has already stated their charge and who has not.* I sat there perfectly still, trying to make myself invisible as I watched the clock slowly tick away.

I listened carefully as each person went, waiting for someone to have a charge worse than mine. As it neared the end of the hour, I would have been happy for anyone to have a charge even remotely as serious as mine. But to my surprise, the worst altercations of these over-tattooed, shaven-headed, muscle-bound dudes only involved a pen or a chair. Given my newly acquired knowledge regarding assaults, I now understood that any of the above items can be considered a deadly weapon if they are used in a forceful manner.

All I could do was wait. Finally, eight o'clock arrived! I was positively jubilant! I had managed to hide during the entire unbearable hour.

Then, the instructor uttered those delightful words, "Well, it is time to go."

We all quickly jumped to our feet. But, my pleasure abruptly ceased when the instructor said, "Wait! There is one more person to go."

This can't be happening. My heart sank and the world seemed to stand still for a few moments. (Note to self: when you perceive that the earth has actually stopped spinning, this is rarely a good thing.) I slowly looked up in disbelief, as the thing I had dreaded minute by minute for the last hour became a reality: she was pointing directly at me.

Fabulous! This meant not only did I have to say my criminal charges out loud, I now had everyone's complete and undivided attention.

The instructor, in her friendly tone, said, "You haven't gone yet. What is your charge?"

"Oh, well, ya know, like an assault," I mumbled.

Assuming my charge was fairly negligible, she said, "An assault, but it wasn't aggravated, was it?"

"Um, technically, yes." I reluctantly replied.

"Well, at least you didn't have a weapon, right?" she said with hesitation. Sensing that I was extremely embarrassed and most assuredly a first-timer, she was doing what she could to help me out.

"Well, kind of," I replied as I simultaneously cleared my throat in a feeble attempt to conceal my response.

Despite her experience, she couldn't hide her surprise. The entire class was now intently listening and staring at me in disbelief. There was murmuring, which I could barely hear over my heart pounding.

She quickly recovered and asked, "Well, what weapon did you have?"

I uttered the two little words that would make me a legend to these people while rendering the instructor speechless: "A Glock."

I could have heard a pin drop in that room. Although I was almost whispering, my voice seemed to boom. I was certain that anyone within a ten-mile radius heard every word.

I feebly protested, "But, I was in my own home."

That precipitated more mumbling.

"Then, why are you here?" she asked as she struggled to comprehend why someone who clearly had never been in any legal trouble in their entire life was pathetically trying to explain what she was now realizing was an extremely serious charge.

"Well, you see, it is a really complicated story. Um, I happened to have the Glock in my hand when I answered the door. I had no idea it was a police officer." My vain attempt to make the incident sound benign was lost on them. It no longer mattered what I said, the damage was done.

The collective gasp they expelled as they threw themselves back against their seats summed the situation up nicely.

One by one their faces underwent a change of expression as they processed what they just heard. The barely five-foot tall blonde they teased about being the teacher was there because of an armed face-off with law enforcement in the harshest jurisdiction in the United States. An actual miniature OK Corral altercation on her front porch, with a Glock no less!

I couldn't seem to stop babbling. "Well, it isn't that big a deal. I mean, it happened so fast. I happened to have it in my hand when the police came to my door . . . ."

I just stopped talking. It didn't matter what I said, their perception of me was forever changed. I was forty-four years old and I had finally attained it: "street cred."

EILEEN STEWART

STREET CRED

FROM THAT DAY FORWARD, MY classmates treated me like a mob boss. Each class they saved me a chair in the middle of the room, with an empty seat on both sides for the requisite body guards. My self-appointed "lieutenants" waited for me in the parking lot before class and escorted me into class and to my designated seat. After class, they escorted me out to my car and watched over me until I pulled away.

My main protector was a man who had been out of jail less than two years for killing another man. Remarkably, he was desperate to have my opinion of his case. Upon hearing the account of the altercation in its entirety, I replied, "That sounds like self defense."

His face lit up and he shouted, "That's what I said!"

We were all strangers bound together by a random judge's order to attend this class. But as each week passed and each person shared a little more of his or her soul, a camaraderie took form. We were merely people who had made mistakes, people who had been wronged and we had allowed that anger to consume us for a few moments too long. There was a solidarity that made our hearts sink with each classmate's disappointment or be heightened by their small victories.

One young man was involved with a stripper. His girlfriend had a terrible temper, and yet, he was the one in trouble as a result of an altercation with her. She was the angry one who beat on him, but inexplicably he was the one in the class. I, of course, shared his frustration. He admitted freely that she was no good for him, but he said that he just couldn't walk away because he was in love with her.

The entire class became protective of him and each class would begin with us asking him if he had managed to gain the strength to leave her. He always said "No," and with that answer, we would all take in a heavy breath and our hearts would go out to him. We had all been there, with a person that we knew was a destructive force in our lives yet our heart couldn't let go.

Some of the reactions were so surprising to me. One woman who rarely spoke finally opened up one night. She was a tiny slip of a thing, with bleach blonde hair and a small face with delicate features. She was talking about her ex-husband, a bully who continually berated her. The tears streamed down her face, and her breath caught as she repeated his favorite taunts: "You are not pretty at all. No one is ever going to want you!"

One of my "lieutenants" was sitting on my right. He sat slumped in his chair, with his long legs jutted out front and arms folded across his chest. Any flesh visible was heavily tattooed, and his unkempt grey, wavy hair hung down, partially covering the requisite biker vest. Upon first inspection, he was no one I would want to meet in a dark alley, the type that would walk in a bar and everyone would fall silent for a few minutes.

His face held its usual bored expression, and it didn't even appear that he was listening. But as soon as he heard her say those words, he dropped his head with such compassion and he uttered, "Man that's cold, really cold."

Over several weeks, he had spoken quite casually of violent physical altercations with little thought, yet when she described the years of verbal abuse she endured, he was genuinely moved.

Eventually, I reluctantly told my story. I recounted how JB had stolen all my property, his six-month affair, and how he had turned my family against me by convincing them I was a junkie. I even included the reason that I took his phone from my neighbors was to allow me to delete my doctor and family numbers from his cell phone. As I explained, I realized how horrific the chain of events sounded.

I lived it and it was still hard for me to believe. JB's cruelty was also beyond the comprehension of my classmates. As a matter of fact, both my "lieutenants" and two of my brand-new biker friends offered to explain to JB the proper way to treat a woman. I do admit I was tempted. But, I told them that it would make me sink to his level, and I refused for him to change who I was. I would however love to be a fly on the wall on Judgment Day when JB tried to justify his actions to God.

I started to wonder about each person in the room and their particular situation. There was a common thread among their stories. They had all been let down by so many people. I couldn't believe the heartache, the lack of people having faith in them. The snap judgments I made when the class began dissipated with each sad story I heard. It was a humbling experience. Yes, I was educated and accomplished. But, who would I be if I'd had the same start as these people?

DIVORCE COURT

DURING THE FIRST FEW MONTHS after being released from the hospital, I regained most of my physical strength and fully recovered my emotional state, all of which I would need to claw my way out of the deep financial hole that JB had created. It would require all the resourcefulness and determination that I had ever possessed.

I had had ongoing discussions with creditors since my release from the hospital and, so far, I had managed to keep the ranch just one step away from foreclosure. I constantly juggled bills to hold on to the property I had left. After finding out that Dee had seized my mail from my mailbox, I opened a P.O. box in town and directed all my mail to it. Each time I walked in the vestibule, key in hand, I was filled with anxiety. My mind wondered what late notices or bank demands awaited me. I drove home before I would allow myself to look at the mail, because the few times I opened it there I broke down in tears. Somehow, the tears stung less when shed in the privacy of my home.

Some of the bills I dreaded the most were from the divorce lawyers. They were so expensive and JB's lawyer continued to correspond with my lawyer over insignificant things. Despite the excessive email exchange between them, we were unable to reach a settlement. Between the fifteen thousand expended to bring the household bills current and the twenty-seven thousand JB had drained from the joint account, he could support a legal battle much longer than I could. I was still out of work on disability, so JB knew I had very little funds to oppose him.

I requested a mediation to try to settle the community property. However, instead of hashing out the division of the property, JB spent the majority of the time telling the arbitrator that my potential earnings far exceeded his, thus he should get the lion's share. JB even made the comment that he wished Texas was an alimony state. After hearing that remark, I directed my divorce attorney to set a court date.

The court date was set in early August. That morning, I awoke with a start, realizing that I would have to face JB. I felt like such a fool. The details that I had discovered over the last few months revealed the depth of his betrayal. I heard my dogs barking and knew Kathy had arrived. I called the dogs inside and locked the front door. I wondered to myself if I would ever be comfortable leaving the dogs outside when I wasn't home. Probably not.

Kathy and I walked into the courthouse. Kathy was the strongest person I'd ever met and simply being in her presence quieted my nerves.

"I know you want this over," Kathy said. "So, what is your bottom bargaining position?"

"All I want is the dining room and those other pieces I bought with my accident settlement money."

"Oh, right. Instead of using that money for bills, you bought that furniture. That way it would last. Didn't you also do an expensive renovation on the house with settlement money?"

"Yes, I did. I replaced all the cheap siding with that expensive HardiePlank and had it beautifully painted to match the new barn. That siding will never have to be replaced. It is cement based. And then, JB ordered all new windows to the tune of like twenty-five grand!"

Kathy looked over at me quickly. "Wait. Do you realize that community property laws divide the increased equity in a home when one or the other owned it prior to the divorce?"

I expelled a long breath. "Oh, yes. I did the research. The only thing that is not community property would have been my accident settlement. But since I spent a total of fifty-one thousand on improvements to the property, he will get half of that anyway!"

She looked over at me and asked, "Do you think . . . ?"

"Now, you are getting the picture. JB ordered the most expensive custom windows they sell. The improvements on my property will have bumped the equity at least seventy thousand dollars. Oh and of course, the twenty-seven thousand I had left in the joint account is gone."

Kathy clenched her teeth. "That means he will wind up with over half of *your* settlement!" Trying to lift my spirits, Kathy said, "Well, wait until that judge hears that JB broke the temporary orders and came and helped himself to all your property when you were not home. The judge should really make him give back the stuff that he didn't have any right to take."

I just nodded. "I would like my lawn tractor returned; I am still paying on it!"

"Yeah, what is up with that? What does a man in an apartment do with a riding mower?"

"A twenty-six-horsepower riding mower to be exact."

Kathy brightened. "Remember what Al said. Al was there when JB and Mitch loaded the moving van. Al said the tractor didn't go on the truck. Mitch drove it down the road to his property. Maybe you can still get it back."

We were both very pragmatic and neither of us believed for a second that I would recover anything. That was over six months ago. Whatever JB didn't use would have been sold by now. My eyes filled with tears. "I know, but after today, I will never have to see or hear from him again. I just want my life back!"

Kathy pulled into the parking lot. She looked over at me and said, "Come on, let's get this over with!"

We went through the metal detectors which seemed normal to me now. We climbed the stairs and started down the hallway looking for the courtroom. When we saw 203 above the door, we pushed it open. I took two steps and then froze. I was stunned. There sat Laney on the front bench, sporting an ear-to-ear grin. She was facing the back of the courtroom—no doubt to catch my expression.

I could feel the color drain from my face. Any confidence or peace of mind I had recovered over the last few months vanished in a matter of seconds. Laney just looked so proud of herself. She added salt to the wound, by treating me to a mock wave, like she was in a parade. I responded to Kathy's tug on my arm and followed her quickly out into the hallway. Laney's laughter faded as I passed through the door.

As we walked into the hall, I turned to Kathy. "What the hell is she doing here? I haven't seen her since that horrific night! That is the last thing I want to be reminded of today."

Kathy reached out to steady my trembling hands. She led me over to the bench. "Audrey, sit down. Take a couple breaths; you can do this. There is nothing Laney can do to hurt you now."

Kathy could not have been more wrong.

When my divorce attorney, Mr. Hargrove, arrived, I ran over to him and pleaded, "Mr. Hargrove, Laney is in the courtroom. Why? I don't need her gloating over how she helped JB run roughshod over me. I was only arrested because she filed criminal trespass charges against me, which were a pile of sh—" Kathy elbowed me, so I didn't finish my sentence.

Mr. Hargrove guided us back over to an unoccupied bench. He reached into his briefcase to retrieve his legal pad. "Hold on, let me check my notes. I was told of a last-minute change. JB wants to have some witnesses testify."

I said in disbelief, "Witnesses? Witnesses to what?" And then it hit me. "JB wants the judge to hear my charges. He is going to make me relive that horrific night. Given my charge, the judge is certainly not going to have any sympathy for me!"

"OK, just calm down. JB has an accusation." He scanned his notes. "Apparently, JB is claiming that you had a murder plot against him, and Laney is going to corroborate that."

"With all due respect, you are not privy to the details of the criminal charges still pending. Laney was the lynch pin of the whole mess! JB can't possibly believe I had any murder plot."

Then I realized why Laney thought it was so amusing. *What a great joke they got over on me again.* "Mr. Hargrove why didn't you call me about this?"

Mr. Hargrove answered, "I am not worried about it. This is a civil litigation, not criminal. It should have no bearing on the division of the property." He consulted his legal pad again. "Unfortunately, it is not just your word against theirs. The email also said that there was another witness, a friend of yours." His fingers quickly scanned the page. "A Linda Whitfield"

My knees started to buckle. They led me back over to the bench, each one of them supporting me on either side. I put my face in my hands. "This can't be happening."

"This is ridiculous," Kathy said. "Call Linda, now!"

With a look of concern, Kathy turned to Mr. Hargrove and led him a few feet away. "Look, I have been staying with her, and there is no way she withstand having JB and that wench telling more lies and tearing her down!"

I pulled my phone from my purse and frantically dialed Linda's number, but just reached her voicemail. I called again every ten minutes but no answer. Maybe they had her hidden in a conference room so I wouldn't have an opportunity to talk to her.

I walked back to Kathy and said, "I can't get ahold of her. This is a disaster!"

"Audrey, Mr. Hargrove said that any criminal case should not be of any consequence." Kathy said, trying to keep her voice even.

"Kathy, the criminal matter has not been disposed of yet. My lawyer has been requesting continuances to demonstrate that it was an isolated incident. If JB and Laney get on that stand and say under oath that I had a murder plot against him, I don't know what harm it could do in the criminal matter. And, I certainly can't testify to anything relating to the incident under oath without my criminal attorney present! I'm screwed!"

"Tell me about this Linda person," Kathy asked quickly.

"Linda is a horse friend; I haven't spoken to her in many months. She doesn't even do my sport; she does dressage."

"Dressage—so she could know Laney?"

"Wow, I didn't put it together. Yes, they would see each other pretty often. I actually met Linda because she is married to a geek. Although, she was at that dressage show that the newspaper article was written about."

"Well, there is no way she can believe you had formed a plot to murder JB. That is ludicrous!" Kathy said with mounting frustration.

"You know what," I said, "I don't know what to believe anymore. Now, understanding the full extent of JB's power of persuasion, it was not beyond the realm of possibilities that he convinced Linda of this ridiculous accusation."

JB was so confident that a judge would sympathize with him because he would introduce my pending charges. My charge was irrelevant to the proceedings, but simply bringing it to the judge's attention would be enough. As far as this county goes, a charge of "aggravated assault with a deadly weapon on a peace officer" was still pending. And, my divorce hearing was in the courthouse adjacent to the same jail where I had been housed less than six months ago. The fact that JB had shown up at my property after he moved to an apartment, and had taken possession of ninety percent of the community property would surely be eclipsed by my charges.

Suddenly, I felt like the same broken soul who lay day after day in that solitary confinement cell, garbed in that filthy jumpsuit atop the two-inch mattress.

Would this nightmare ever end?

I knew what listening to hours of JB and Laney's accounts and the criminal record being introduced would do to me. I turned to Mr. Hargrove. "Forget it. It is not worth it. They win again." I dropped my head in defeat. Any fight I had left was gone.

The final settlement left me with all of the community debt, to the tune of about sixty thousand dollars, and no reimbursement for the six months of bills that were in arrears. I was not granted any property except for the few items that JB left behind. I didn't know how I was going to recover financially, but I would, somehow. I ordered myself not to cry to no avail.

Kathy and I walked towards the parking lot. "Well, it is finally over," she said through clenched teeth.

She made a great effort not to show her contempt for both JB and Laney, but I could tell she was fuming underneath. We had originally planned to go out for a lunch celebration that I was finally free of JB, but neither of us was in the mood.

On the drive home, Kathy reached over and grabbed my hand. "Audrey, just think of the good; you will never have to deal with JB again. That alone is almost worth the money!"

I gave her a withering look.

Kathy said sheepishly, "Too soon?"

"Uh—yeah."

"OK, sorry. Audrey, your animals lived through it; the rest can be replaced."

Kathy was right, of course. My animals couldn't be replaced; furniture could. Maybe someday I would fully regain my dignity. I was mortified by Mr. Hargrove's statements that there was an accusation of a murder plot and two potential witnesses to corroborate the allegation. I am sure it was a first for Mr. Hargrove, but he was professional enough to hide his discomfort.

EILEEN STEWART

THE LAST PIECES
OF THE PUZZLE

THE NEXT MORNING, I AWOKE with a start, my mind filled with the disturbing image of Laney wearing that smug smile, sitting in the first row of the courtroom. I lay there thinking about the events of yesterday. The initial shock of the ludicrous allegation had dissipated, but something continued to nag at me.

That's it! Yes, it was Laney's smile. It was exactly like the self-satisfied smile that JB had the night of that horrific assault. As if they were both in on some nefarious joke, some big secret. The fact that Laney was actually prepared to swear under oath in front of a judge that I had concocted a murder plot against JB opened up other possibilities. It made me wonder if it was an isolated incident. *Were there other times Laney had defamed me in an effort to support JB?*

The irregularities of the so-called "Super Bowl party" came flooding back. Now that I understood the lengths Laney would go to support JB in divorce court, what latitude might she take in the privacy of her home? This put the details surrounding that night in a completely different light. My assumption had always been that JB had gone to Mitch and Laney's house during the two hours he pretended to go break the apartment lease. He had to burn time somewhere—there was no way to rescind the lease at that stage. Certainly, JB played up the mistreated victim in a loveless marriage chained to a mentally ill wife. Perhaps he told them that I wouldn't even let him have few personal effects before I threw him out. Whatever JB told them it was most assuredly designed to fuel the fire.

Given his wild claims in divorce court yesterday, was it possible that JB would have gone as far as insinuating that I was dangerous? Did he suggest I could become violent?

Even if JB had alluded to that, I was certain Laney didn't believe any such thing. I was aware that she harbored a great deal of jealousy for my horse expertise and more prominent technical position, but I was astonished by the extent to which she was willing to help JB. I didn't believe for a second that she thought I was capable of formulating and carrying out a murder against anyone. However, Laney's jealousy would make it easy for her to envision JB as the victim.

Suddenly, a snippet of conversation with Dr. Walden replayed in my mind. The recollection of the conversation was so vivid, it was as if I were sitting in his office. I was telling him about the stress of competition, and how personally people would take it when they lost. The intense jealousy that can arise between competitors within a particular sport. I had told him that Laney had trained for dressage the entire time I had known her.

Dr. Walden had said, "Wow, that is quite a time commitment. Does she do well?"

"Well, she struggles with it. Competition is very hard. People work for many years to excel at a particular discipline."

Dr. Walden: "Do you have much success in competitions?"

I replied, "I have worked my way up to national level shows in a few events . . . "

"Do people take it seriously—I mean, personally—if they do not win?"

"Oh, yeah. It can get dicey at any level." Then I told him about the girl who had unhooked my trailer after the show.

Dr. Walden looked at his pad. "So, you can probably share war stories with Laney. Is there any rivalry between you and Laney?"

Then I told him about the clinic with the Olympian and the happy hour at the end of the day. I remembered saying, "Well, she had gone to a lot of trouble to put on the clinic and that probably wasn't the way she expected the day to end."

That was years ago. Then there was that schooling show and the full-page newspaper article my father framed for a gift.

I remembered the paper needed photos, and they directed me to go back to the barn with a photographer, which caused quite a stir. Laney knew boarders at that stable quite well. I actually had to borrow the same equipment and do the same maneuvers to provide pictures for the article.

I threw back the covers and walked out to the living room. I walked over to the wall to read the framed article. I hadn't read it in years. Wow, it even included what my reiner competitor friend said about beating people at their own game. The last few lines of the article had quoted him saying, "I just read a book on *How to Win Friends and Influence People* – and that ain't it!"

I remembered Dr. Walden catching the parallel with the clinic at Laney's house and that schooling show. "Mister T. Isn't that the horse you mentioned before?"

Oh wow! Mister T and Linda! Linda was the one I asked to read the pattern to me when I was showing Mister T! Is that why Laney thought of her to be another witness? That article had been hanging on my living room wall for years. Did Laney interpret that as a dig?

During those two lost hours, did they devise a plan on how to "handle me" if I came to the party? Something to further discredit me or to send me into an even deeper depression? Was Laney finally going to get to see me knocked off 'my high horse?'

At first, I chastised myself for such an outlandish notion. Yet, the more I contemplated it, the more plausible it seemed. It would not have been difficult if all three of them stuck to the same story. They could just tell my potential attacker that given "previous behavior" they fully expected the estranged wife to become "unhinged." I had tried to find out information about him after the attack. Someone told a friend of mine that he was an out of state ex-cop. That would explain why I had never seen him or heard his name before. They could say that they would appreciate if he would be on hand in case of an "unfortunate altercation." Particularly, because JB had just moved out the day before.

I hadn't considered that before. Why did JB wait almost two weeks after he rented an apartment to tell me he was leaving me?

JB had convinced my own surgeon that I was not in pain. I had no idea what JB had told Mitch and Laney over the last few months. It actually didn't matter; whether Laney really expected me to be violent or pretended to be, the result was the same. The stranger would be wary of me and expect trouble from the minute I entered the room. He had no other information to go by.

JB had convinced Dad and Bonnie that I was an addict before my plane had touched down. As a result, every move I made was scrutinized and blown out of proportion to fit JB's narrative.

His plan worked flawlessly over Christmas. Was it possible he had repeated his cruel trick?

I thought back to the beginning of that terrible night. I had noticed something was off as soon as I pulled in Laney's driveway. I had expected a scene like their usual Super Bowl parties—the outside lights ablaze, seeing people huddled around the big-screen TV through the front glass windows. But, there was no noise, no chatter, no loud praising or chastising players as I exited my truck. I remembered thinking: It's already well into the second quarter; where is everyone?

Was that why the front room was dark and all the outside lights were out? So, no one would drop in unexpectedly to watch the game? Particularly, someone who could decide for themselves without being subjected to JB's spectacular web of deceit?

I replayed my conversation with Mitch just hours before the events of that fateful night. He stated that he had to hurry home after playing golf to help with the big party. For the first time, I concentrated on his tone and not the words. His voice was odd, like he was nervous. If he didn't want me to come to the party, why mention it? Mitch and Laney had continued to pretend to be my friends. I called him because he had offered to unload the shavings. My call was not a surprise to him. Not at all.

I had confided in JB after Christmas that my family abandonment was far more painful than all the physical pain combined. I replayed the images from the so-called party in my mind. JB had taken great care to position himself so that he would be the first person I would see. JB had a front-row seat to the moment of my bitter realization that the last two friends I had left were actually in his camp. I had just stood there, frozen, my expression crumbling. It shook me to my core.

It was surreal; everyone was watching me as if I had three heads. No one moved a muscle; they just stared at me wide eyed. I could picture Laney with the baby on her lap. But Laney's arms were not wrapped around her. Her hands were jammed down into the cushions. Laney refused to take the phone I was holding out for her. This raised more questions.

If Laney was afraid of me, wouldn't she wrap her arms around her child? Maybe turn her back to me in the chair and shelter the baby. Why have the infant next to the door at all? At least be in the back of the room, if it was safety she desired.

I remembered the self-satisfied smile on JB's face as my attacker jerked me off the ground and threw me against the wall. Once I had taken two steps in the room, the stranger had jerked me up like a rag doll. If my attacker expected an altercation, that would explain why he didn't hesitate for even a second. Why he sat spring-loaded in the corner chair, waiting for the bell.

Was JB hoping this final betrayal would completely destroy me? But if I took pills this time, no one would be there to dial 911.

This was all conjecture and difficult to prove. However, it answered all of the questions that had been plaguing me since that awful night, and even a few more I hadn't noticed at the time. It felt good to finally have a working theory that was both logical and explained all the anomalies.

THE CONTRACT

HOLLY, A DEAR FRIEND OF mine, heard what happened and called me out of the blue to have lunch with her. She told me to meet her at a restaurant only ten minutes from my ranch. I was very happy to see her; it had been almost a year since we had seen each other. Holly's eyes revealed her shock at how different I looked.

I grabbed her hand gently and said, "I'm OK. How are you?"

"Apparently doing a lot better than you." Holly said. "I know how much you love your ranch. Are you going to be able to hold onto it?"

"Well, I have been working with the bank," I said. "I am still way behind, but I have had that mortgage for almost twenty years and this is the first time I've ever been behind on the loan. I am having to really shuffle around bills, but I am managing to hold on."

"Well are you going to be super happy with me! I think I found a job for you. I found this on a career website. You need to go win this contract!"

She slid the two-page document over to my side of the table. I scanned the page quickly. "Holly, come on. I am not qualified for this. I have done this type of work, but not anything at this level. The biggest project I have ever worked on had a budget of just under four million dollars." I looked down and read the description again. "This program has a budget of nearly two hundred million dollars! Holly, you're kidding, right?"

"Audrey," she said, "look at the hourly rate. That's more than twice your normal salary. I talked to Kathy. It will take a miracle to save your ranch. Now, go convince them you can do this job!"

I slowly read the job description again and shook my head.

"Audrey, you have worked for me before, so I know you have what you need to get this job done. You are going to have to bust your butt, but you can do this. From what Kathy told me, you have been arrested, almost got shot on your front porch, wound up in solitary confinement, and then did a stint in the maximum-security ward of a psychiatric hospital. It can't be worse than that."

I knew she was right. I absolutely needed this. A high-paying contract was my only chance to not just postpone the foreclosure but to actually bring the account current. It was a six-month contract, so the rate was very high. I had no idea how I was going to sell this, but I had no choice. I had to try.

A few days later, I went in to meet with the Program Director of the immense project. I was so nervous and talked so fast, that I had no idea what I actually said. Whatever I said, it worked! I was scheduled to go into their human resources office the following day to fill out the application. I called Holly to thank her on the way home.

I had no clue how I could succeed at this job, but I would do everything I could to hold on to this contract. I went to the desk they said was mine, sat down and went to work. This project was so enormous and specialized that they flew over two hundred consultants from all over the world each week. I was amazed at the caliber of these people; they were extremely talented. I was honored to be a part of this team. Every day was an absolute battle, but I continued to reach and stretch to keep up with these world-class consultants.

The Program Director would bark an order and I would nod my head and say, "No problem."

When the Program Director left the room, the consultant next to me would say quietly, "Do you know how to do that?"

I would say defiantly, "No idea, but I will by five o'clock."

I was quick on my feet and carefully watched everything the other consultants did. They were incredibly nice and they helped me when I needed it. Maybe they saw past my manufactured bravado and somehow sensed that this contract was critical to my survival.

I was very mindful never to allude to anything regarding my divorce or my brief tangle with our beloved judicial system. I didn't dare allow myself to think about it. I couldn't afford the distraction. Twice a month, I covertly slipped into or out of the side door at the courthouse to see my probation officer. Each time mortified that a co-worker would see me. I still couldn't wrap my head around the events of the last year, so it certainly wasn't a conversation I wanted to have with my new colleagues.

At the end of each day, I walked across the parking lot to my car, astounded that I had made it through another day. With a huge sigh of relief, I'd slide into my car and head home to my ranch. Gradually, I began to believe that I had a chance of holding on to it. Each day that passed and I met the demands of that job, I regained a little more of my former self.

TYING THINGS UP

DURING THE LAST YEAR, MY life had been in such turmoil that I had to differentiate between lawyers if I told someone to call my attorney. Requiring the services of a divorce attorney was bad enough, but to also be in need of a criminal attorney was overwhelming. Both my divorce attorney and my criminal attorney met me the first time when I was in the lowest point of my life. I was frail, emaciated, and only partially lucid after sleep deprivation. But thank God, they gave me a chance. Maybe I looked so pitiful neither one of them could walk away. They both left the hospital vowing to help me in any way they could.

The last time I saw my divorce attorney, he just looked at me and shook his head. I was in my tailored pinstripe suit, leather briefcase in hand, on the way to give a presentation to the Board of Directors.

"What?" I asked.

"I can't believe you are the same person. I told my assistant that you are a testament to the human spirit!"

I flashed a smile as I climbed in my sleek black import.

Ross Moran's strategy as my criminal attorney had been simple but effective. Mr. Moran told me to just remain a model citizen and he would keep asking for continuances. Mr. Moran said that the police had no idea what to think at the time because it was such a confusing set of circumstances and they were at a loss as to what to do with me. He said that every week that went by without incident demonstrated that the psychotic break was not only an isolated incident, but the direct result of the medication, not a mental defect.

The first day we met, he had patiently listened to my original story about the "setup" and the assault at the supposed Super Bowl party. The story probably didn't make any sense given the state I was in. I remember scribbling on paper to show him how Laney's property was laid out in a hodgepodge fashion. Then, I circled the area on the crude drawing to indicate where my husband's car was parked and how it was almost hidden back by the barn. I struggled to explain the events in a rational manner but I can't imagine how it sounded. I think he believed there was some basis to it, because in all our subsequent conversations, I had never once wavered from my original story. I could fill in more detail as my mind cleared, but my description of the events was always the same.

"I know what you said," Mr. Moran said, "and I am not saying I don't believe you. But, I need to be realistic. This is what I know: if your husband and his friends are willing to stick to that story, then it is just your word against theirs. They all signed affidavits and it is a felony to sign a false complaint. So, my guess is they will take that story to the grave! Besides that, to refute that they gave you a criminal trespass warning to stay off their property two years prior would be extremely difficult. Particularly if they will back each other up. It is just not worth it."

I reluctantly nodded my head.

"Don't get me wrong. I know that whatever really happened certainly wasn't fair to you. But, I also I agree with your divorce attorney. I can't believe you are the same person I met in the hospital. Things are going great for you. You have recovered your career and have a more lucrative and prominent position than you have ever held. I recommend we concentrate our efforts on moving forward."

So, I made a trek each month to appear in court to request yet another continuance. It was a hassle to miss three hours of work once a month but his strategy was working, as evidenced by the judge's expression gradually softening. My continued appearance in court, respectfully dressed and gainfully employed was conveying the point that was critical to my defense strategy.

Ross Moran was a very wise man. There was nothing wrong with my mental state and it was best to let time demonstrate that. Eventually, they would come to their own conclusion, that without a cruel husband working the psychiatrist like a puppet, none of this would have ever happened—that had to be good enough. As Mr. Moran predicted, I was given a disposition of deferred adjudication to a misdemeanor with two-year probation.

Days turned into weeks. Weeks turned into months, and within six months, I was current on the mortgage again. I couldn't believe it; I had literally saved the ranch! I would never recover the property or money I lost as a result of the divorce, but I wouldn't allow myself to think about it. I focused on what was positive: I was alive, I still had my ranch and all my animals were safe. My contract was renewed twice, which gave me almost two years at the contractor rate, allowing me to gradually recover my financial state.

EILEEN STEWART

WHAT IS WRONG WITH THIS PICTURE?

THERE WAS ONE COURT APPEARANCE that was more memorable than the others. It summed up the way I felt during the last several months, like my world was upside down. It started out like every other court appearance. When hearing my name called as the next one on the docket, I walked up and stood before the judge. I carefully lined my feet up with the bright red line that was taped to the carpet for this very purpose. As always, my lawyer was at my side and did all the talking. Despite the number of times I appeared, my heart still raced and my stomach lurched with the knowledge that my fate was no longer determined by me. The judge had the exclusive power to remedy my life or destroy it, with one pound of the gavel.

Once again, another continuance was granted, which meant I had another month to continue my life before going to trial. As we turned and walked to the back of the courtroom, Mr. Moran leaned down and whispered to me to wait for him outside. Assuming that he had another client to represent, I pushed open the heavy wooden door and walked to the closest bench. To pass the time, I casually watched the people who walked by and noticed another soul sitting alone on the bench directly across from me.

We covertly studied each other with interest and quickly diverted our eyes when we sensed that our voyeurism was discovered. I reached down and straightened the seam on my pinstriped slacks and adjusted the matching jacket for something to do.

I noted my hallmate's long lanky frame, slumped lazily on the hard wooden bench. His white tank top exposed his heavily muscled arms and assorted tattoos. His teeth were bright white in contrast to the ebony skin tautly stretched across his young features. His jeans were torn and frayed at the bottom, and the long shiny chain attached to his wallet hung loosely down below the bench. His hair cut was neat and short, with the added flair of initials fashioned by a shaver across the top right quadrant of his head. He had a kind expression and seemed to sense my discomfort from across the hall. After several minutes passed, we gave up the pretense that we were not curious about the other. He spoke first.

He said sheepishly, "Uh . . . Excuse me, but did I just see you come out of felony court?"

I gave a barely perceptible nod as I willed myself to disappear.

He said kindly, "Oh. So, you were there for a friend?"

I said quietly, "Um well, not really. It was for my charge."

He just shrugged as if to say he understood. I was so grateful he didn't ask the actual charge that brought me to this courthouse each month.

In an effort to be both polite and divert the conversation, I asked, "Were you in there too?"

He said quickly, "Nah, I was in misdemeanor court."

I said, "Oh, did it turn out OK?"

He replied, "Yes, although it was for my friend. I was just there for support."

At that we both laughed; there was no pretending this situation wasn't comical. Among my many lessons on this journey, the one that was so prevalent was to not judge a book by its cover. Something we were both guilty of that day.

FORGIVENESS

THINGS WERE NEVER QUITE THE same with my family after that dreadful Christmas. My father and I spoke but there was a strain in our relationship. It really bothered me, so when my father came down to visit, I decided to address it. He was very impressed with my consultant engagement; therefore, I was on good footing to discuss the level of JB's deception. My father was never the "talk it out" type and would have preferred that it was never mentioned again. But, I needed him to look me in the eye and hear what happened. I finally convinced him to sit down and talk about it. But every time I told him about yet another horrific event, he shot out of his chair and walked away from the table.

"Sit down, Dad," I ordered. "I am trying with every fiber of my being to forgive you, but you have to understand what I went through!"

"I can't listen; it is so awful."

I shot back through clenched jaws, "Well, I lived it, so you are going to hear it. Sit down!"

It took three hours to tell the gruesome tale. Eventually, he heard it all. Both of us cried, but we got through it. And because he truly listened and owned how appallingly he had let me down, I was able to forgive him. He showed me that he had really taken it to heart and accepted responsibility the next time we went to dinner with Kathy and Arnie. Dad literally had his hat in his hand when he spoke.

"Thank you so much for what you did," said my father somberly. "I should have done it, but I didn't. Thank God my daughter has friends like you!"

He then grabbed Kathy in a hug and shook Arnie's hand. My father was a very proud man, and I know that took everything he had. About a year after that, he was diagnosed with the early stages of Parkinson's disease. I am so glad that we were able to talk it all out while he could truly appreciate what I had endured.

THE END

AUNT MARLYN CALLED TO TELL me that my father had suffered a severe stroke. I rushed down the hospital corridor, with no idea of what to expect.

My father was not a very big man in stature, but he commanded respect. Now, he looked so small and thin as he lay among the crumpled white sheets in the hospital bed. His skin was almost translucent, his hands balled up like an infant.

"Dad, it's me," I said softly.

I turned to Aunt Marlyn.

"You know what I can't figure out?" I asked.

"What, sweetie?" she said gently.

"It has been several years since all that mess with the divorce and the criminal charges. Yet, not one person asks me about it. And, it just occurred to me that it felt like how it was with Mom."

"What do you mean?" she asked.

"Well, I remember growing up that no one ever mentioned my mother. No one said one word. It now seems really strange to me. It was as if she never existed."

"Well, when your father didn't want to talk about something, nobody talked about it."

"What was my mother like?"

"Patsy? Oh, I loved her!" Aunt Marlyn said as she ran her hand up the crease of her slacks. She chuckled a little bit to herself, reliving a memory from long ago. Then she turned and looked at me. "Well, she's you, Audrey. Put on a brown wig and there you have it. You have her smile, her laugh, even the inflection of her voice. She lit up any room she was in. Just like you," she said as she stroked my hair.

"I always felt sad that no one ever spoke of her, like people erased her from their minds, like she wasn't worth remembering. I guess I feel a little like that now, like people have chosen not to acknowledge those events, like it is too taboo to even discuss. I guess things haven't really changed that much. I was in jail, solitary confinement, and then a psychiatric hospital! I was facing twenty years! But not one question about the disposition, about how the case was resolved. Not one!" I turned to her and said, "You don't find that strange?"

We ended the conversation just as Bonnie briskly swept into the room in that matter-of-fact way she always had.

She glanced at Dad and said, "Mac. It's Bonnie. How are you today, hmmm?"

Just then the nurse walked by.

Bonnie said, "Excuse me."

The nurse stopped and popped her head into the room.

"Has he had a bowel movement today?" Bonnie asked.

I clenched my jaws and looked at my father lying so helplessly in that bed.

"Bonnie," I said, "can I talk to you in the hall for a minute?"

She looked at me quizzically. "What is it?"

"It will just take a second." I motioned my head towards the hallway. We went a few steps out in the hallway and I said, "Bonnie, can you please ask his nurses about his BMs in the hall? Does it have to be in front of him?"

"He can't hear us," Bonnie snapped.

"What if he can? My father was a judge, an intelligent and respected man. Why not do it just in case."

My relationship with Bonnie had been strained ever since that infamous Christmas. Since I was pretty sure that without my dad around, I was permanently off the guest list, I glared right back at her. This was my dad, and no one was going to disrespect him like that.

I had a different perspective. I had been the person that became invisible, who people stopped caring what they said around. I remember the things JB said when I only had auditory senses, the looks people gave me, the side glances at what I said.

The nurses could see my discomfort and they made a deal with me. I would visit Dad during the night and watch TV with him. One evening we were watching TV, just him and me.

"Dad?"

He worked to focus his dull blue eyes on me.

"Patsy?"

"No, Dad. It's me." Patsy was his nickname for my mother. I picked up his gnarled cold hand and encircled it with my two hands. "It's Audrey"

He nodded perceptively and slowly closed his eyes.

That was when it finally became crystal clear. When my father looked at me, he didn't see me—he saw Patsy!

So many years of me wondering why nothing I did was good enough. So many times, I tried to figure out what I did wrong, and why he was disappointed with me. Now, it all made sense. She was broken, and he couldn't fix her. He was a smart man, a very smart man, and yet he was powerless to save her from herself. She was the love of his life, the mother of his children, and she left him holding the bag. And every time he looked at me, it all came back.

"Dad, I need you to concentrate really hard."

His dull blue eyes found their way across the ceiling and seemed to actually see mine.

"I am OK now. I am at the top of my game professionally. I saved my ranch. I can even ride again. Dad, I have my life back. It's over. I forgive you. Please don't live this way for me."

Three hours later, my father passed away. But as I had just had a brief visit, I knew exactly where he was going. My heart was full; my father was finally at peace.

About the Author

EILEEN STEWART HAS been a technical professional for thirty years, but the greater part of her life has been her passion for horses. As a result of a car accident, she endured several spinal surgeries and the accompanying pain and depression. Shortly thereafter, Eileen became the victim of a psychiatrist who overprescribed mind-altering drugs that further deteriorated her fragile emotional state. Despite a bleak prognosis, due to a little ranch gelding's patience and unwavering encouragement, she has returned to competition. For those precious moments when she is riding, she is 'whole' again.

People can easily sympathize with the pain of physical injury, but emotional suffering is far from understood. Understanding the incredible healing powers of horses, Eileen has founded a non-profit organization, A Helping Hoof, which utilizes rescue horses to assist Veterans with their difficult transition to civilian life. There are many Veterans who are standing on American soil, but they have yet to come 'home'.

Helping Hoof is a collaborated effort of American horse people working together to show their appreciation for a Veteran's great sacrifice. A Helping Hoof is a 501c3 and currently in initial phases (www.helpinghoof.com). This program will provide the medical attention and professional training necessary to recover abused and neglected horses. Therefore, these horses will get a permanent home, and will never suffer again. In turn, the Veteran's quality of life will be greatly enhanced. In essence they will save each other.